THE KEYS
to Strategies for Language Instruction

Engagement, Relevance,
Critical Thinking, Collaboration

LESLIE GRAHN AND DAVE McALPINE
Foreword by Greg Duncan

The American Council on the Teaching of Foreign Languages
1001 North Fairfax Street, Suite 200
Alexandria, VA 22314

Donna Clementi, Content Editor

Graphic Design by Goulah Design Group, Inc.

ISBN: 978-0-9896532-7-5

Foreword

If schooling is about preparing people to live productive lives as adults, then educators must equip learners with the dispositions and skills that will enable them to be life-long learners. They need to experience the exhilaration and joy that can come from acquiring new knowledge and skills, and they need to be led by skillful instructors who know and value the importance of learner-centered education—instructors who position learners to be agents of their own educational destinies.

Leslie Grahn and Dave McAlpine present just the right tools at just the right time to help world language educators operationalize the shift to learner-centered and learner-driven instruction. *The Keys to Strategies for Language Instruction* has the potential to change how instructors operate in fundamental ways.

Grahn and McAlpine's work springs out of, and is an extension of, the ever-growing body of scholarship on the importance of the teacher in the learning equation. They underscore that it is what the teacher *does*—not just what the teacher knows—that makes the biggest difference in how successful learners are. They emphasize, through the various chapters of the book, the need for instructors to possess a wide variety of strategies that can be used across an array of activities, and they devote substantial time and space to modeling the kind of thinking skillful instructors employ to make important decisions about how learning can best be facilitated. Each chapter includes the opportunity for readers to analyze sample scenarios that pose a challenge and then to ponder different ways of addressing them. The authors also suggest strategies that instructors can use to apply information gleaned from each chapter as well as additional resources that can inform their work.

Readers are invited into the topic of each chapter by being given access to the brain trust that is the collection of ACTFL Teachers of the Year. These outstanding educators in our field reach deep into their thoughts and experiences to provide provocative and insightful statements that both frame the content of each chapter and make us want to read more.

Anyone familiar with the literature on teacher effectiveness will see the immediate parallels between the current research and Grahn and McAlpine's work, making this contribution to world language education completely in-sync with broad trends in effective educational practice for today's learners. This parallelism makes it possible for language instructors to see themselves within a broader context as valuable contributors to an educational experience that can make a big difference for learners and their futures.

How learners practice using the target language in class positively influences how well they communicate in real-life situations. *The Keys to Strategies for Language Instruction* puts powerful tools in the hands of K–12 language educators who seek to make classroom practice meaningful and purposeful with the goal of increasing the proficiency of language learners.

Greg Duncan
Founder and President
InterPrep, Inc.

Introduction

Essential question: What criteria guide the selection of instructional strategies for this ACTFL Keys publication?

Effective teaching strategies activate students' curiosity about a class topic, engage students in learning, develop critical thinking skills, keep students on task, engender sustained and useful classroom interaction, and, in general, enable and enhance the learning of course content.

(Boundless, 2015)

Strategies are "ideas for how to give students the practice that will make it possible for them to achieve the course goals…what you will have students do in order to learn the course content **and** practice the goals" (Tewksbury & McDonald, 2017). The intent of this *Keys* publication is to suggest language learning strategies that move learners towards greater proficiency in a world language. It follows ACTFL's *The Keys to Assessing Language Performance* (Sandrock, 2010), and *The Keys to Planning for Learning* (Clementi & Terrill, 2013). Sandrock provides guidance on how to design assessments, the starting point for all instructional planning as recommended by Wiggins and McTighe in *Understanding by Design* (1998). Clementi and Terrill continue the process by providing templates that facilitate the planning of standards-based thematic instructional units, lesson plans, and curricula. *The Keys to Strategies for Language Instruction* (Grahn & McAlpine, 2017) completes the trilogy by focusing on effective strategies to build proficiency through learner-centered instruction.

Clementi and Terrill suggest in *The Keys to Planning for Learning* (2013) that unit and lesson design respect five basic principles, first identified by Helena Curtain (2010) in her work with young language learners. Effective units or lessons are:

- Communicatively purposeful: Building continuously toward greater proficiency;
- Culturally focused: Deepening cultural knowledge and understandings;
- Intrinsically interesting: Relevant to learners' lives now and in the future;
- Cognitively engaging: Requiring critical thinking skills;
- Standards-based: Reflecting world-readiness goals for learning languages.

Each of these principles is also relevant to the selection of appropriate instructional strategies that build intercultural communication skills.

Organization of the Book

The Keys to Strategies for Language Instruction includes five chapters. Chapter One discusses the changing roles of instructors and learners in the 21st-century classroom. Chapter Two focuses on creating a language- and culture-rich environment. Chapter Three outlines strategies to strengthen performance in the three modes of communication. Chapter Four describes strategies that foster independence and collaboration among learners. Chapter Five suggests ways to evaluate the effectiveness of the strategies in building learners' communication skills and in deepening their cultural understandings, preparing them to be active participants in the global community.

To facilitate selection of effective strategies when planning lessons and units, we offer an Instructional Decisions Guide.

Key to Instructional Decisions

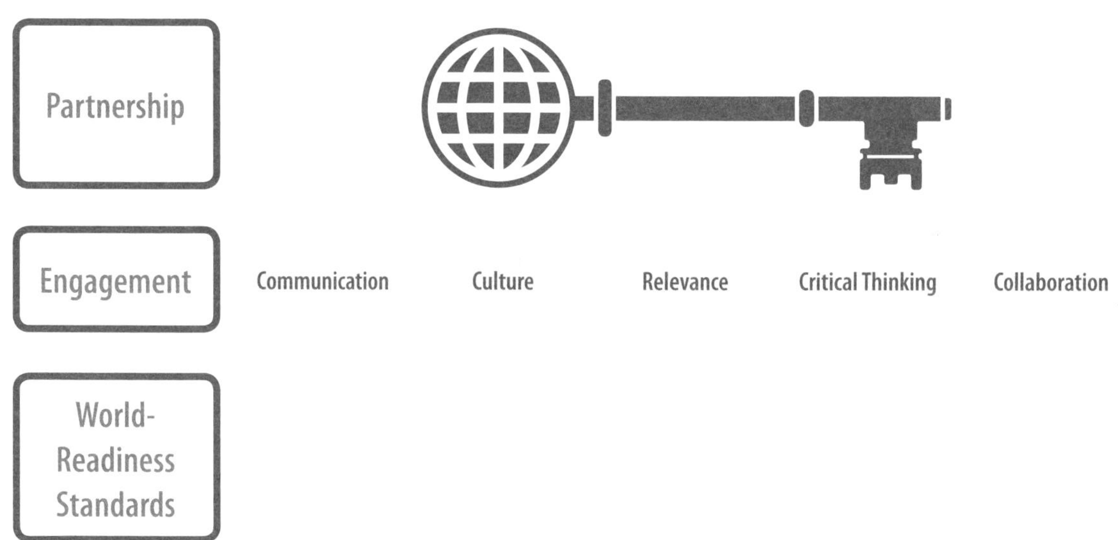

The handle of the key has three parts: the center block, *Engagement*, reminds us that the active interest and participation of the learners is essential for learning to take place. Above *Engagement* is *Partnership*. Instructors and learners explore themes and topics together in a partnership to discover new knowledge and understandings while simultaneously building communication skills in the target language. The box below *Engagement* is the *World-Readiness Standards*. The Standards identify the broad goals for learning world languages. Together, the three components in the handle of the key provide the foundation for the selection of instructional strategies. Moving from a teacher-centered to a learner-centered classroom requires instructors to work with learners in a partnership, gradually giving learners more control of what they are learning, how they are learning, and how they evaluate their learning, fostering more learner engagement. The topics that learners explore reflect the goal areas of the World-Readiness Standards deepening learners' knowledge and understanding of the target language and the people who speak that language while, at the same time, increasing learners' understanding of themselves and the world.

To the right of the handle is the blade of the key with five elements that are important to consider in the design of every lesson: *Communication*, *Culture*, *Relevance*, *Critical Thinking*, and *Collaboration*. These five elements are reflected directly or indirectly in every chapter in this publication. *Communication* and *Culture* are at the heart of our discipline. Instruction in a world language class is designed to give learners opportunities to practice communicating with respect and sensitivity in the language they are learning, and to deepen their understanding of the people and cultures associated with that language. *Relevance* influences a learner's motivation to continue building communication skills in the target language. Language learning takes time that today's learners are willing to give only if what they are learning is relevant to their lives now or in the future. *Critical thinking* engages learners' brains as they explore new topics, try to find answers to essential questions, create new understandings of topics they are learning about, and solve problems creatively. *Collaboration* gives learners opportunities to practice speaking spontaneously and purposefully in face-to-face interactions in class, and virtually with people around the world to complete a project, solve a problem, exchange information and/or share ideas in a discussion.

These criteria are reinforced by our combined experiences as K–12 and post-secondary educators. We believe they will resonate with world language instructors at all levels. While some of the strategies may need adaptation to the age and language level of the learner, all are designed to increase learners' capacity and confidence in understanding and communicating with respect in a world language. This publication provides the key to selecting instructional strategies that engage all learners in building their intercultural communication skills in the world languages they are learning.

At the end of each chapter are icons that identify opportunities to actively engage with the concepts and ideas presented in the chapter:

Reflect on the essential question: Write your thoughts related to the question before, during, and after reading each chapter.

Analyze an example that applies the content knowledge to the classroom.

Apply ideas to your practice using the knowledge gained from the chapter.

Extend your learning by completing these activities.

Deepen your knowledge by exploring additional resources.

It is our hope that the ideas presented in this publication, while by no means exhaustive, will open discussions about how to build proficiency in world languages at all levels using effective instructional strategies.

Acknowledgments

We would like to begin by thanking ACTFL for teaming us up for this project. Through our work on this project, we were able to achieve a K–16 blend of our diverse experiences and backgrounds.

For both of us, the ideas and strategies we have shared in this book are a product of our respective bodies of work in the profession. We would like to thank all of our colleagues who have supported us, taught us, collaborated with us, and expanded our thinking as language educators at the school, institutional, state, regional, and national levels. Special recognition goes to our colleagues, mentors, and friends in the Northeast region, including those in Howard County Public Schools, the Maryland Foreign Language Association, and Northeast Conference on Teaching Foreign Languages, and to those in the Central region, including the University of Arkansas at Little Rock, the Arkansas Foreign Language Teachers Association, and the Central States Conference on the Teaching of Foreign Languages, among many others who share our passion for the work.

In the process of writing *The Keys to Strategies for Language Instruction,* we appreciate the help we received from Paul Sandrock, Director of Education at ACTFL, who mentored and shepherded us through the completion of the book. We would also like to thank our early reviewers, Paula Patrick and Donna Clementi, whose insights and suggestions were very helpful to us. A special thank-you to Donna Clementi, who provided her expertise to the final edits of this edition. She offered both encouragement and a critical eye in the final stages of the manuscript.

Finally, a very special thanks goes to our families, who are our sources of constant support and encouragement.

—Leslie Grahn and Dave McAlpine

Table of Contents

Chapter 1 Facilitating Instructor-Learner Partnerships for Learning

How Has the Relationship Between Instructors and Learners Evolved in the 21st Century?

- Instructors and Learners Working Together to Strengthen 21st-Century Literacies
- Instructors and Learners Working Together to Set Learning Goals

"I subscribe to the ancient philosophy that Plutarch stated in his teachings: 'The mind is not a vessel to be filled but a fire to be kindled.' As a world language teacher, I cannot imagine a better model to follow. Language teachers are charged with fostering an intercultural understanding as well as igniting the intellectual flames of adolescents—one student at a time. As an 18-year teaching veteran, I seek to fulfill this challenge by cultivating a positive rapport with students and fomenting an atmosphere in my classes in which both student and teacher strive to be exemplary."

—Ken Stewart, ACTFL Teacher of the Year 2006

Instruction in the 21st century is profoundly influenced by a round-the-clock access to information made possible by advances in technology. The learners in classrooms today, most born after the year 2000, have never known a world without the Internet. Their generation is often known as the "iGeneration" or the "Founders" or the "Builders." Although the name for this generation is yet to be finalized, the characteristics that unite this age group are clear. Relevance is critical for the members of this generation in terms of what they want to learn, both for their own personal interest and for active involvement in the global community. They share many similarities with the Millennials that preceded them. They use the Internet constantly day and night to connect with people and search for information. They expect to use technology as a means of learning, and they expect what they learn to be relevant to their lives. They want choice in what they learn and in how they demonstrate achievement of learning. In contrast to this emphasis on individual exploration, Millennials and Builders are also very social, enjoying opportunities to work together in small groups on projects, both in person and virtually to discover new knowledge and understandings. They value open frameworks, open platforms, and open sources for sharing and collaboration. "Crucially, this new learning is heavily based in the "real-world" of action and problem solving, and it is enabled and greatly accelerated by innovations in digital technology. These forces converge to produce deep learning tasks and outcomes" (Barber, 2014). To meet the needs of these increasingly independent learners, the relationship between instructor and learner is changing from instructor as provider of knowledge and learners as receivers to a genuine partnership between instructor and learner as they explore new knowledge and set goals for learning together.

Instructors and Learners Working Together to Strengthen 21st-Century Literacies

Technology is ubiquitous in day-to-day transactions and interactions. It is particularly important to world language learners, providing a myriad of opportunities to practice the language they are learning in real-time, real-world contexts. Technology can now connect language learners to native speakers right from their classrooms. What could be more real-world and relevant for learners than using the language they are studying to videochat with people who speak the language they are learning? What could be more real-world and relevant than exploring websites about topics ranging from current events to pop culture to virtual tours of places around the world where the target language is spoken? Together instructors and learners explore the Internet to deepen their understanding of the language and topics they are studying. ACTFL developed a position statement in 2017 on the role of technology in world language instruction. It states in part:

> The use of technology is not a goal in and of itself; rather technology is one tool that supports language learners as they use the target language in culturally appropriate ways to accomplish authentic tasks. Further, all language learning opportunities whether facilitated through technology or in a classroom setting, should be standards-based, instructor-designed, learner-centered, and aimed at developing proficiency in the target language through interactive, meaningful, and cognitively engaging learning experiences. ... The development of technology is best driven by the needs of the language learner, supporting the kinds of interactions our students need to become college, career, life, and world-ready (ACTFL 2017a).

Let's consider how technology can effectively support teaching and learning in world language classrooms. The SAMR model (Figure 1), developed by Ruben Puentedura (2010), describes four levels of technology integration. These range from substitution, which is simply using a tech tool to complete a task that was originally completed without technology, to redefinition, which transforms the task into a more engaging learning experience.

Figure 1. SAMR Model by Puentedura (2010)

SUBSTITUTION Technology acts as a direct substitute, with no functional change	ENHANCEMENT
AUGMENTATION Technology acts as a direct substitute, with functional improvement	
MODIFICATION Technology allows for significant task redesign	TRANSFORMATION
REDEFINITION Technology allows for the creation of new tasks, previously inconceivable	

At the lowest level—*substitution*—technology is used with no substantial advantage to the learning process. For example, an instructor replaces a chart about forms of transportation in Austria, normally drawn on the chalkboard or whiteboard, with the same chart electronically displayed via an interactive whiteboard. The lesson is taught exactly as it would be taught were there no technology. If the interactive whiteboard is used exclusively as a *substitution* for chalkboards and whiteboards, the interactive potential of the device has not been exploited to engage the learners. Technology has not enhanced the learning experience.

The same lesson related to different forms of transportation in Austria can be *augmented* using the interactive whiteboard's connections to the Internet. Authentic video clips, photos and headlines from cities in Austria bring the topic to life. An instructor can take the entire class on a virtual trip on the Austrian Railjet (Kaemena360, 2017). Placing the lesson in an up-to-date real-world context increases interest and motivation among learners (ACTFL 2017a).

Technology can prompt significant redesign or *modification* of the lesson. For example, Italian language learners who are completing a unit on how Italians define healthy eating can go beyond the information in their textbook, using the Internet to research the slow-food movement in Italy. They can find out how popular the slow-food movement is among Italian families by videochatting with classrooms in Italy. The classrooms might then collaborate on a project suggesting ways to encourage participation in the slow-food movement in both Italy and the United States.

Finally, technology allows for *redefinition* of tasks, creating new tasks that are difficult if not impossible to accomplish without technology. Via technology, an instructor can now lead Arabic language learners on a virtual tour of the pyramids in Egypt, pairing Google Cardboard viewers with cellphones and the Expeditions app from Google. They can "walk together around the pyramids" to see them from different angles, stopping to discuss how and why the pyramids were built. Imagine how the conversations change when learners feel like they are in Egypt. A virtual tour such as this becomes "the next best thing to being there." This is one example of the new paradigm where learners and instructors become partners in mutual discovery, creation, and use of technology to spark meaningful conversations based on real world texts, situations, and interactions. Technology's influence on how people communicate is reflected in Figure 2, showing Marc Prensky's comparison of the literate person of yesterday, today and tomorrow (2012).

Figure 2. Prensky's comparison of the literate person across time (2012)

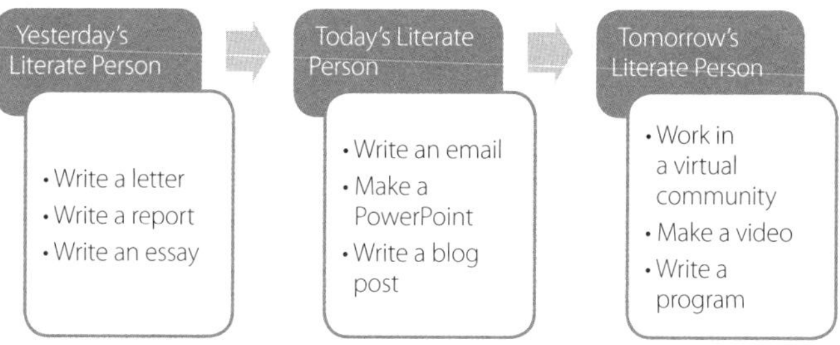

In 2013 the National Council of Teachers of English expanded the definition of literacy for the 21st century. Reading and writing remain foundational, but technology greatly expands access to a wide variety of texts, and makes it possible for learners to share their ideas with a global audience. According to this revised definition of literacy, active, successful participants in this 21st-century global society must be able to:

- Develop proficiency and fluency with the tools of technology;
- Build intentional cross-cultural connections and relationships with others so as to pose and solve problems collaboratively and strengthen independent thought;
- Design and share information for global communities to meet a variety of purposes;
- Manage, analyze, and synthesize multiple streams of simultaneous information;
- Create, critique, analyze, and evaluate multimedia texts;
- Attend to the ethical responsibilities required by these complex environments.

These 21st-century literacies and their application to world language learning are explored in depth at ACTFL's Languages and Literacy Collaboration Center (tinyurl.com/LLCCACTFL).

The implication is clear: technology, effectively integrated into instructional units, prepares learners for successful communication in a globally connected world. Table 1 (see p. 6) includes examples of how instructors can plan activities using technology purposefully to build communication skills among learners.

The following example illustrates how a university Spanish professor designed several tasks where learners practice their communication skills using a variety of technologies. To enhance the textbook unit on student life in Spanish-speaking countries, he assigned the following tasks:

- **Task One:** Learners read an online article from *Diario21*, a daily newspaper from the state of Guerrero, Mexico, concerning the disappearance of some 210 students between the years 2010-2014. They write their personal summaries of the article, responding to instructor prompts, and post them on the class Wiki for comment (Interpretive and Interpersonal Modes).
- **Task Two:** Learners connect with Mexican university learners from their list of online videochat pals and ask them several questions about student life at the university. They also ask about the disappearance of the students in Mexico (Interpersonal Mode).
- **Task Three:** Learners create a Wordle to display the most commonly used vocabulary words they acquired in their readings and from the interviews with the students in Mexico. Half of the class prepares a digital recording in the form of a news program about the information they have learned during their research. The other half of the class uses a newsletter template from a digital writing program to create a newspaper article about the information they have learned. The products are shared with other Spanish classes and with the students they interviewed at the Mexican university.

The tasks created by the Spanish professor illustrate the purposeful use of technology within and outside of class. The professor used his expertise to help learners locate and evaluate authentic resources, and to connect with native speakers. He also gave continuous feedback including "just-in-time" instruction on how to use certain structures and vocabulary to improve communication. Learners used what they learned about the unit theme and topic, along with their knowledge of digital tools, to create new understandings to share with audiences beyond the classroom.

Here is another example for younger learners: Spanish language classes in a middle school in Wisconsin became interested in the needs of a small community in Nicaragua through a partner city relationship. Originally started as a pen-pal activity, the middle-school Spanish classes wrote letters and sent photos to their counterparts in Nicaragua. A group of volunteers carried the letters to Nicaragua, and carried back responses along with photos of the Nicaraguan students. Friendships were formed and letters continued to be exchanged, albeit slowly, until the

Table 1. Purposeful activities using technology

Activity	Description	Modes of Communication	Examples
Electronic pen pals	Learners correspond with a pen pal from a target language country	Interpersonal Interpretive	Gmail Skype Instant messaging
Ebooks	Learners read or listen to ebooks online in the target language	Interpretive	International Children's Digital Library (http://en.childrenslibrary.org/)
Learner-made recordings of performances	Learners record a speaking performance using an online platform or app which may include animation	Presentational	Vocaroo Voki Blabberize Audacity
Online class discussions	Learners participate in a forum or blog to discuss topics related to class	Interpersonal Interpretive Presentational	Wikispaces Edmodo Voicethread
Digital comic strips	Learners create a digital comic strip using an online generator or app	Presentational	Toon Doo Make Beliefs Comix
Online articles and websites	Learners read online articles and/or websites in the target language	Interpretive	BBC World Newseum Newsela Paperboy
Mindmapping/ Brainstorming	Learners use brainstorming software, platforms, or apps to brainstorm ideas either individually or collaboratively	Presentational	Inspiration/Kidspiration Spicy Nodes Padlet Mindmeister Wordle Tagxedo
Cultural Presentations	Learners use websites, software, or apps to create a presentation about the target culture	Presentational	Powerpoint Prezi Glogster Keynote Anyflip Google Cardboard
Voicemail	Learners leave audio messages for a classmate or the instructor in the target language	Presentational	Google Voice Most message programs on smart phones
Digital stories	Learners create digital stories and story books	Presentational	Storybird Show Me Educreations Zoo Burst

Internet arrived in this small community in the mountains. Today, the learners in Wisconsin and Nicaragua can connect via videoconference with each other and even exchange text messages, asking and responding to questions about each other's lives. Instructors work as partners with the learners, helping them compose biographies to share, create survey questions about life in Nicaragua, and prepare interview questions to ask during videochat connections. Each year, the Wisconsin middle schoolers determine ways they can help the Nicaraguan community based on interviews they conduct with the volunteers who travel to Nicaragua, with Nicaraguans who visit Wisconsin, and with their videochat and text-messaging buddies. These connections over the years resulted in projects to collect books, medical supplies, garden supplies, and sewing supplies. Many of these projects would never have been imagined by the middle schoolers without the exchanges, both virtual and in person. Ongoing support for this small community has continued for more than a decade.

These two examples used a combination of learning within and outside the classroom. Blended learning, mixing face-to-face interaction in a classroom with tasks that the learners complete independently or via online collaboration, can be used effectively to increase opportunities for learners to use the target language to complete real-world tasks. In the first example, the university students conducted real-time interviews with students in Mexico to collect additional information about a current issue in Mexico. In the second example, middle schoolers used videochat and texting to exchange information with learners in Nicaragua. In both examples, technology enabled learners in their classrooms in the United States to exchange information with their peers around the world, making real-world connections using the target language, connecting communication with culture, relevance, critical thinking, and collaboration.

Other ways learners can work independently outside the classroom to reinforce and enrich their language skills include:

- Exploring the Internet, using search engines specific to countries where the target language is spoken, to find information relevant to the topic they are studying;
- Creating written and oral presentations using appropriate media to share new knowledge and understandings with audiences beyond the classroom;
- Practicing conversation skills with native speakers of the language through global connections such as MyLanguageExchange.com;
- Improving their accuracy in listening, speaking, reading, and writing through on-line skill-building websites such as Duolingo.com (free) or Babbel.com (paid subscription required).

Cognizant of all these opportunities, instructors need to be sensitive to learners' access to and experiences with technology. Regular access to technology may not be readily available to all learners. That means instructors may have to do more full-class presentations, sharing authentic video, audio, visual, and written resources. Paper copies may have to be made available to learners who don't have Internet access at home. Instructors may have to provide class time in a computer lab to show learners how to access and use online resources or certain technology tools. Providing learners with websites that include tutorials on how to use a variety of technology tools allows learners to explore these tools independently. An example of a website with tutorials is Novastartalk, developed by the Northern Virginia Community College (http://novastartalk.nvcc.edu/). If your school or program offers after-school language clubs, participants could come together to learn how to use technology tools, to share websites related to the target language, and/or to create presentations using technology tools. Helping learners access and use technology responsibly is critical to their development of literacy in the 21st century in both their native language and languages they are learning.

"The real transformation of technology and the Web is that it creates a freedom to learn and a freedom to contribute and participate on a global scale that didn't exist even a decade ago" (Fullan & Langworthy, 2014, Page 2).

> IDEA-SHARING
> Imagine you have ten minutes to address the governing board of your school or the University Foundations Board to convince them to fund technology for the world languages program. Using the information in this section, identify five reasons for them to invest in your department.

Instructors and Learners Working Together to Set Learning Goals

The transition of the relationship between instructor and learners to a partnership in learning acknowledges that instructional goals are not solely the instructor's responsibility. As stated at the beginning of this chapter, today's learners want choice in what they learn and in how they demonstrate achievement of learning. While instructors are accountable for meeting approved curricular goals of the institution where they work, they are also keenly aware that learners will be more successful if they have input into setting the goals, and if the goals are personally relevant to them. "Human action is caused by purpose, and for action to take place, goals have to be set and pursued by choice." (Moeller quoting Locke and Latham (1990) in LinguaFolio®.) A successful partnership between instructor and learner is critical, as they work together to set goals for learning.

Research related to goal-setting shows that learners are more committed to working toward goals when the goals are specific, proximal, and moderately challenging (Bandura, 1986; Locke & Latham, 1990, 2002). The introduction of LinguaFolio®

by the National Council of State Supervisors for Languages (NCSSFL) in 2003 facilitates goal-setting in the world language classroom. "LinguaFolio® is a proficiency-based, learner-directed formative assessment tool for setting and achieving language goals" (www.NCSSFL.org). It is patterned after the European Language Portfolio (ELP). LinguaFolio® has three components:

- **A Learner Biography:** a record of personal language-learning history that helps learners set goals and reflect on their language learning and intercultural experiences. This section includes the NCSSFL-ACTFL Can-Do Statements, reflecting the ACTFL proficiency levels and sublevels.
- **A Dossier:** a place for learners to collect evidence of their language learning progress, including samples of work showing achievement of each can-do statement.
- **A Passport:** a journal of experiences learning different languages and reflections about those experiences.

In 2014, NCSSFL collaborated with ACTFL to connect LinguaFolio® with ACTFL's Proficiency Guidelines to create the *NCSSFL-ACTFL Can-Do Statements*, available as a free download at www.actfl.org. The *NCSSFL-ACTFL Can-Do Statements* were originally intended for use by learners to help them set their personal communication goals, and then monitor their progress toward meeting those goals. Today the Can-Do Statements serve as a useful tool for instructors as well as learners:

> "The Can-Do Statements help learners identify what they need to do to function at a specific level of proficiency. The statements also help educators plan curriculum, units of instruction, and daily lessons to help learners improve their performance and reach a targeted level of proficiency. Through multiple opportunities to show what they "can do" in classroom formative and summative assessments, unit by unit, learners collect the evidence that points towards a specific proficiency level. The proof that a learner has reached a proficiency level occurs through an independent assessment of proficiency such as the ACTFL Oral Proficiency Interview or Writing Proficiency Test."

The NCSSFL-ACTFL Can-Do document includes Can-Do Proficiency Benchmarks that describe what learners "can do" at the Novice, Intermediate, Advanced, Superior, and Distinguished Proficiency levels. The Proficiency Benchmarks are organized by the modes of (Interpersonal, Interpretive, Presentational) and for Intercultural Communication. For each of the benchmarks, there are examples of specific Can-Do Performance Indicators that reflect the mode and the level of performance. It is important to remember that the examples are meant to serve as models to help instructors and learners write their own Can-Do statements specific to the content of the instructional unit they are studying. The examples in the *NCSSFL-ACTFL Can-Do Statements* illustrate the kinds of performances that are appropriate for each mode and level, and are not intended to be used as the content for a curriculum. Table 2 includes three examples from the *NCSSFL-ACTFL Can-Do Statements*. The Mode and Level are identified, followed by the Proficiency Benchmark for that mode and level. The final column includes a Can-Do Performance Indicator that reflects the Proficiency Benchmark. In the same box is an example of how instructors and learners might customize the Performance Indicator to reflect the unit they are studying.

Instructors and learners can use the Can-Do statements as a starting point for sharing responsibility in setting learning goals. As stated earlier, the instructor is responsible for planning lessons to meet the learning goals and course requirements mandated by the school or institution. However, giving learners choice in how to meet those requirements is motivating, encourages perseverance, and leads to higher overall performance (Patall, Cooper, & Robinson, 2008). Researchers caution instructors to limit the number of choices learners are given. The same study showed that giving learners more than five options has a negative impact on the learner's motivation, perseverance, and performance.

Here is an example of how a high school Spanish teacher guided her third-year class in writing Can-Do statements that reflected the required curriculum goals targeting the Intermediate Low level and integrating learner choice. The required curriculum listed as one of the learning goals: Learners will be able to present the biography of a well-known person from the Spanish-speaking world. This learning goal also included specific language functions learners needed to demonstrate as part of the process of preparing to present the biography. Among the functions was *asking and answering informational questions*, signaling an Interpersonal task. Learners began by individually choosing a field of personal interest from a list of options: music, sports, science, cinema, politics. In consultation with their teacher, they selected a well-known person to investigate and created customized Can-Do statements. For this unit, one of the Interpersonal Can-Do statements a learner created combined the required language function

Table 2. Sample Can-Do Statements

MODE	LEVEL	PROFICIENCY BENCHMARK	PERFORMANCE INDICATOR WITH EXAMPLE
Interpretive	Novice Mid	Novice: I can identify the general topic and some basic information in both very familiar and everyday contexts by recognized practiced or memorized words, phrases, and simple sentences in texts that are spoken, written, or signed.	I can identify some basic facts from memorized words and phrases when they are supported by gestures or visuals in conversations. *Customized for a unit "My School":* • I can understand when my friends greet me at school.
Presentational	Intermediate Mid	Intermediate: I can communicate information, make presentations, and express my thoughts about familiar topics, using sentences and series of connected sentences through spoken, written, or signed language.	I can give straightforward presentations on a variety of familiar topics and some concrete topics I have researched, using sentences and series of connected sentences. *Customized for a unit "Biodiversity":* • I can write a short article comparing Earth Day in the U.S. to Earth Day in Switzerland.
Interpersonal	Advanced Mid	Advanced: I can maintain spontaneous spoken, written, or signed conversations and discussions across various time frames on familiar, as well as unfamiliar, concrete topics, using series of connected sentences and probing questions.	I can maintain discussions on a wide variety of familiar and unfamiliar concrete topics of personal and general interest, and sometimes academic, social or professional topics, by using probing questions and providing detailed responses across major time frames. *Customized for a unit "Planning for the Future":* • I can share with others what the U.S. can learn from other countries about how to make post-secondary education in the United States accessible and affordable for all.

(*I can ask and respond to informational questions*) with the learner's personal choice related to a required learning goal (*about Antonio Banderas, an international film star from Spain*), resulting in: *I can ask and respond to informational questions about Antonio Banderas, an international film star from Spain.* Other learners wrote similar Can-Do statements that reflected their choices of well-known people from the Spanish-speaking world. While the learners were exploring, individually or in pairs and small groups, the well-known people they had identified, the teacher monitored their work to inform the selection of strategies and learning experiences to help learners achieve the unit learning goals. Throughout the instructional unit, the teacher offered ongoing opportunities for learners to assess their progress toward reaching the unit goals and to gather evidence that they had achieved the unit "Can-Do" statements. The teacher gave ongoing feedback to the learners on the quality of their evidence, suggesting where more practice or improvements were needed, and ultimately confirming achievement of the learning goals.

IDEA-SHARING

The Can-Do statements are not intended to be used as checklists. Instead, the Can-Do statements from the three modes of Communication work together to prepare the learners to meet the required curricular learning goals. Share ideas for Can-Do statements in the Interpretive and Presentational Modes at the Intermediate Low level. These ideas might be used as models of what learners "can do" in this unit about well-known people from the Spanish-speaking world.

Well-crafted Can-Do statements are specific and closely related to the unit learning goals, with performance expectations that challenge the learners slightly beyond what they can currently do with ease. *The NCSSFL/ACTFL Can-Do Proficiency Benchmarks Chart* (Appendix B) is particularly helpful to learners in writing Can-Do statements, because it represents an overview of the progression toward greater proficiency from Novice to Intermediate and beyond across all modes of communication. When referencing the Proficiency Benchmark chart, it is important to remind learners that they need multiple examples of their performance at each level to demonstrate what they can do.

In addition to LinguaFolio®, there are several generic platforms for designing digital portfolios where the *NCSSFL/ACTFL Can-Do Proficiency Benchmarks* can be incorporated to document language learning progress. Among the ones frequently mentioned by world language instructors are Evernote, Google Sites, Weebly, and WordPress. Again, the instructor's role is that of facilitator, selecting and introducing the platform to the learners, explaining the purpose and how to use the selected platform. It is the learners' responsibility to maintain the portfolio, identifying learning goals and associated Can-Do statements, selecting evidence to document achievement of the goals, and reflecting on the learning process.

Digital badging is another way to document learners' skills and knowledge. Badges are awarded to learners who demonstrate achievement of knowledge and skills that reflect the goals for a course or other learning experience. More information is available at the National Language Resource Center at the University of Texas (https://openbadges.coerll.utexas.edu/) or at Open Badges (OpenBadges.org).

In addition to the Can-Do Statements that describe performance at each level of proficiency, the approximate amount of time needed to perform with competence and confidence at each level is also an important consideration. To help establish realistic yet challenging language learning goals, it is helpful to combine the Can-Do Proficiency Benchmarks with a chart such as the one in Figure 3. Figure 3 shows expected performance levels for language learners in programs where learners meet at least three times a week for a total of 90 minutes each week.

Another ACTFL document, *Oral Proficiency Levels in the Workplace* (ACTFL), presents the proficiency level required for success in a variety of jobs, and the associated language preparation needed. To underline the importance of time in learning a new language, Lightbown (2016) compares the amount of time children from birth to six years of age are immersed in their first language (approximately 15,000 – 20,000 hours) to classroom instruction time when the world language is taught as a course during the school day (approximately 180 hours/year). She reminds us that we have precious little time to build proficiency in a second language, even in immersion or dual language programs (approximately 540 – 900 hours/year). Instructional time at the university level may be even less and, thus, increases the importance of maximizing the use of classroom time, both inside and outside of class. Lightbown believes that making good use of classroom time cannot be overstated. Instructors must thoughtfully and purposefully select strategies and activities to maximize opportunities for learners to interact in the target language. Lightbown's imperative is to make every minute count.

Figure 3. Expected performance levels of world language learners (ACTFL Performance Descriptors 2015)

Time as a critical component for developing language performance

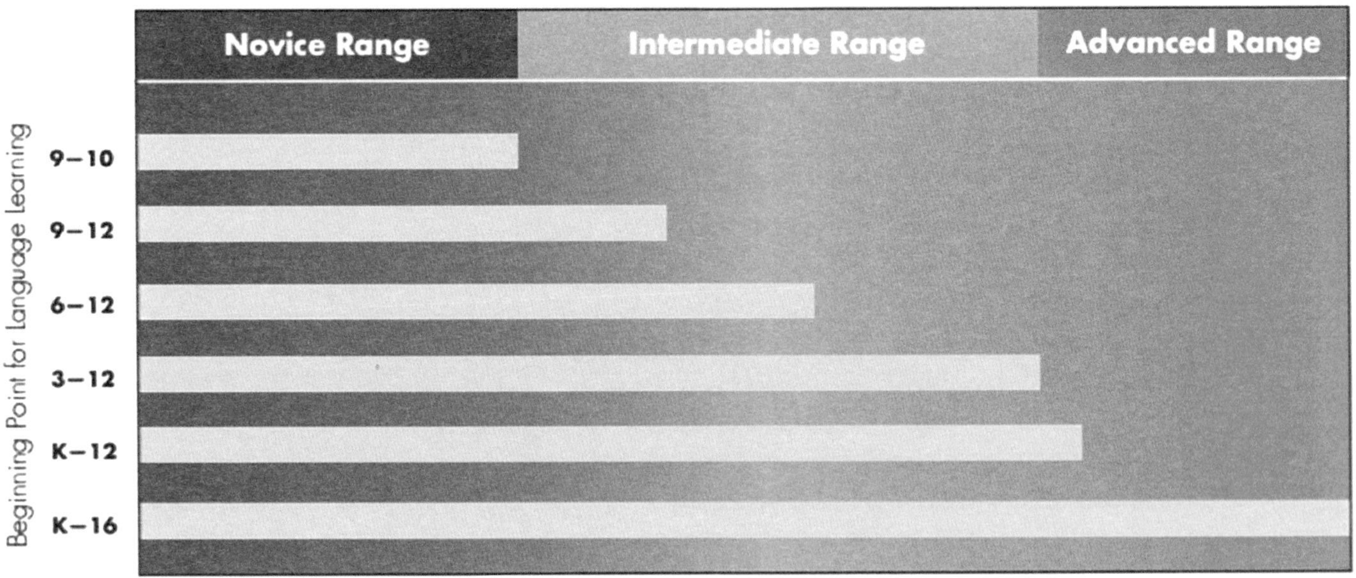

Summary: Learners today thrive in classrooms where they are partners with their instructors in exploring topics relevant to their lives now and in the future. Technology provides access to a seemingly endless library of information, allowing learners to investigate topics in depth, and to pursue topics of personal interest. Instructors use their expertise and background knowledge to help learners effectively search for information. They show learners how to evaluate the credibility of the information they find. They offer suggestions on tools to organize information, and to present ideas to audiences locally and globally. All of these skills contribute to the development of learners' 21st-century literacies. Learners and instructors also work in a partnership to set learning goals and to evaluate the achievement of those goals. Course requirements are mandatory. Giving learners choice in how to meet those requirements is motivating, encourages perseverance, and leads to higher overall performance. Clearly written Can-Do statements empower learners to monitor their own progress and collect evidence that shows what they can do. They can engage in meaningful conversations with their instructors about their progress and, in partnership, identify the next steps they need to take to continue their progress toward proficiency.

Reflect on the essential question: How has the relationship between instructors and learners evolved in the 21st century?

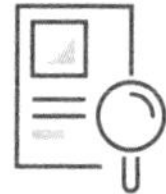

Analyze an example of an unfinished unit plan and suggest Can-Do statements that learners can customize to reflect personal choices in meeting the unit goals. Refer to page 19 in this chapter for a model.

The Essential Question for the unit is: Why can't all young people go to school? The unit is designed for high-school learners in a third-year French class. The targeted proficiency level is: Intermediate Low. The teacher has identified five goals for this unit.

Learners will be able to:

- Describe the current status of education of young people locally, nationally, and globally;
- Identify and categorize economic, political, and social reasons why young people around the world cannot go to/stay in school;
- Give reasons why going to school is important to oneself and locally, nationally, globally;
- Give examples of initiatives to support schooling for all young people around the world;
- Connect with a school in (x) to learn more about the school and the number of students who graduate compared to the number who started school but did not graduate.

Apply ideas to your practice using the knowledge gained from the chapter.

1. How can you integrate effective use of technology into your instructional practices?
2. How can the NCSSFL/ACTFL Can-Do Statements help you and your learners achieve the established curricular goals for a unit of instruction?

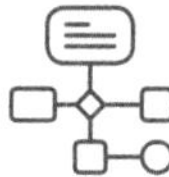

Extend your learning by completing these activities.

1. Investigate the recommended technologies and class scenarios in the ACTFL World Languages 21st-Century Skills Map (ACTFL, 2011).
2. Ask colleagues which technology tools they find most helpful and how they use them.
3. Do a web search for apps for cellphones and tablets appropriate for classroom use.
4. Investigate your school, school district, or university policy on acceptable use of technology.
5. Explore the LinguaFolio® Training Modules for ideas on how to use the NCSSFL/ACTFL Can-Do Statements at http://www.learnnc.org/lp/editions/linguafolio.

Deepen your knowledge by exploring additional resources.

Digital Portfolios

Cummins, P. W., & Davesne, C. (2009). Using electronic portfolios for second language assessment. *The Modern Language Journal*, *93*, 848–867.

Laine, C. (2013) Creating a world language portfolio with Google Drive. Retrieved from https://www.youtube.com/watch?v=_cHcwcPZ6Y8

Goal-setting

Dörnyei, Z., & Ushioda, E. (2013). *Teaching and researching: Motivation.* Routledge.

Moeller, A. J., & Yu, F. (2015). NCSSFL-ACTFL Can-Do Statements: An effective tool for improving language learning within and outside the classroom. *Dimension*, *50*, 69.

Roman, S. N., & Soriano, S. A. (2015). Autonomous learning and self-assessment through the European Language Portfolio (ELP): A pilot study on primary education. *The Journal of Language Teaching and Learning*, *5*(2), 37-53.

Technology

Kramsch, C. (2014). Teaching foreign languages in an era of globalization: Introduction. *The Modern Language Journal*, *98*(1), 296-311.

Yang, S., & Chen, J. (2014). Fostering foreign language learning through technology enhanced intercultural projects. *Language Learning and Technology*, *18*(1), 57-75.

Chapter 2 Creating a Language- and Culture-Rich, Safe Learning Environment

How Does the Classroom Environment Influence Language Learning?

- Creating an Immersive Atmosphere for Learning
- Maximizing the Use of the Target Language
- Creating a Safe Environment for Learning
- Establishing a Well-Managed Classroom
- Creating a 'Cognitively Busy' Classroom

"I must build a community of learners based on trust and integrity. I must be clear that the classroom is a real place to learn, create, explore and be honored, as well as being shared space for all. The classroom must be a microcosm of the multilingual and multicultural world of which I speak and aligned to the values of language and culture learning to which I adhere."

—*Toni Theisen, ACTFL Teacher of the Year 2009*

When learners cross the threshold into a world language classroom, either virtually or in person, they are entering a place where talking with classmates (in the target language) is encouraged rather than discouraged, where making mistakes is a valued part of learning to communicate effectively, and where creativity is nurtured as learners are transported via their imagination to places where the target language is spoken.

Creating an Immersive Atmosphere for Learning

Whether learners are participating in person or virtually, it is important that they feel surrounded by the target language and culture. Having a classroom dedicated to the language being taught is very important to learning. It serves as a sort of cultural island where the target language is heard, seen, and used, creating an immersive atmosphere for learning.

For learners, the immersive environment begins right at the door where the instructor greets them with "Bonjour," "Hola," or "Nihao." Music from the target cultures may be playing quietly in the background to welcome them each day. Or perhaps a video clip about current events or popular culture is playing for them to view as they are getting ready for class to begin. There might be an authentic image related to the day's lesson projected on a screen with a task that engages the learners immediately in using the target language. All of these options encourage the learners to switch their brains from English to the target language.

The physical arrangement of desks or tables in the classroom sends a strong message about the importance of learners working together. Turning the desks or tables in such a way to allow learners to face one another allows for natural, face-to-face communication. There is no lost time when, after modeling by the instructor, the learners are asked to "turn and talk" to discuss an idea, respond to a question, or practice new vocabulary or a new sentence pattern. There needs to be enough space around the desks or tables to allow learners to get up and move around to talk to other classmates, or to form lines, circles, or small groups for activities and games. Space around the desks or tables also facilitates instructor movement to monitor the interactions among the learners for continuous use of the target language, to model a correct sentence pattern or vocabulary item, and to give feedback on individual, pair, or group work.

In an optimal situation, the world language classroom has enough space for stations where learners can access video, video games, audiobooks, language practice activities, games, artifacts from the target cultures, etc., during independent learning time. There is also a place where learners can browse through authentic texts in the form of both fiction and nonfiction books, magazines, newspapers, comic books, brochures, maps, etc. A space where props and costumes can be quickly accessed helps bring a conversation or story or cultural situation (ordering in a café, visiting a museum, recreating a historic event) to life. Everything is neatly organized and labeled, making it easy for learners to find and use them.

The walls of the world language classroom are also important in the creation of an immersive environment. Charts showing new vocabulary, question patterns, or ways to ask for clarification help learners stay in the target language as they try to express their thoughts and ideas. Posters highlight the places and cultures associated with the target language. Examples of learners' work are displayed for others to see. A designated space where objectives and a sequence of activities are posted daily helps learners stay on task and understand the purpose for various activities in which they will participate. A world map is useful to situate the geographic location of a lesson or unit of instruction. Consider posting current events from countries that speak the target language near the map as another way to make the language relevant. Displaying the World-Readiness Standards serves as a constant reminder of the overarching goals for learning a world language. Posting both the Can-Do Proficiency Benchmarks Chart (Appendix B), and the poster, *What Language Learners with a Growth Mindset Do* (Figure 4), keeps learners focused on the journey to increased proficiency.

All the elements described above work together to create a language- and culture-rich environment for world language learners where they can immerse themselves in the target language and related cultures.

Those teaching at colleges and universities cannot usually meet all of the suggestions given for creating a language- and culture-rich environment, but attempting any one or a few of the suggestions will help establish that the classroom is a place where the new language is valued and is the path that will lead them to proficiency.

IDEA-SHARING

Having a growth mindset is important to building independence among learners. How would you encourage learners to practice the strategies listed on the growth mindset poster? (Figure 4)

Maximizing the Use of the Target Language

The American Council on the Teaching of Foreign Languages (ACTFL) issued a position statement on the use of the target language in the world language classroom in 2010. It states:

> Research indicates that effective language instruction must provide significant levels of meaningful communication* and interactive feedback in the target language in order for students to develop language and cultural proficiency. The pivotal role of target-language interaction in language learning is emphasized in the K–16 *Standards for Foreign Language Learning in the 21st Century* (NSFLEP, 2006). ACTFL therefore recommends that language educators and their students use the target language as exclusively as possible (90%+) at all levels of instruction during instructional time and, when feasible, beyond the classroom. In classrooms that feature maximum target-language use, instructors use a variety of strategies to facilitate comprehension and support meaning making. For example, they:
>
> 1. Provide comprehensible input that is directed toward communicative goals;
> 2. Make meaning clear through body language, gestures, and visual support;
> 3. Conduct comprehension checks to ensure understanding;
> 4. Negotiate meaning with students and encourage negotiation among students;
> 5. Elicit talk that increases in fluency, accuracy, and complexity over time;
> 6. Encourage self-expression and spontaneous use of language;
> 7. Teach students strategies for requesting clarification and assistance when faced with comprehension difficulties; and
> 8. Offer feedback to assist and improve students' ability to interact orally in the target language.

Figure 4. What Language Learners with a Growth Mindset Do

* Communication for a classical language refers to an emphasis on reading ability and for American Sign Language (ASL) to signed communicative ability (ACTFL, 2010).

At the beginning of a course, learners must understand that the best way to learn to speak a language is to hear and use the language as much as possible. This is true for both instructor and learners. To that end, the instructor uses the target language continuously combined with lots of gestures, visuals, and repetition to make sure learners understand the main idea of what the instructor is saying. The instructor's responsibility is to make sure that the learners understand what is being said. It is the learners' responsibility to follow the instructor's cues to understand first the main idea, and gradually more details of what is being said. The learners need to be reassured that the instructor will keep checking to make sure they understand the big ideas, and that it is acceptable not to understand every single word. The amount of target language that learners understand and use will continue to grow over time.

Hearing the instructor speak the target language continuously can be overwhelming for some learners. Here are some ways that instructors build confidence among all learners to actively participate in 90+% use of the target language. Select one option or a combination of options to establish communication in the target language as the expectation for interactions among learners and instructors:

1. At the end of the first day of class where the target language was used continuously, the instructor may take a few minutes to switch to English to explain to the learners that, by staying in the target language, their own understanding and ability to use the target language will grow more quickly. Give the learners some tips on how to be "detectives," picking up clues to understanding the target language. Reassure them that you will make sure they understand the "big ideas" and that you will not let them get lost. Teach a couple of simple phrases ("Repeat, please"; "Show me, please") or a signal to give learners "lifelines" to let the instructor know if they don't understand. In K–12 schools you might send a letter home to parents explaining how you will help their children learn to understand and communicate in the target language. In post-secondary institutions, one might send the same information to academic advisors and others that regularly have contact with your learners.
2. Keep a sign in the front of the classroom indicating the target language on one side and English on the other. English can be spoken only when the sign is turned to English, and both learners and the instructor have to ask permission to turn the sign to English. The switch to English should be brief, and should always be followed by turning the sign and returning to the target language. This intentional pause and break from the target language disciplines both the instructor and the learners to avoid code-switching at random times. It also allows the brain time to switch how it is processing the messages.
3. Set incremental time goals for staying in the target language if a class lacks confidence in their ability to understand the message. Ask the learners to focus for five minutes on listening and indicating through gestures what they understand, and set a timer. Gradually increase the amount of time and build in opportunities for learners to respond in the target language until the whole class period is in the target language. At that point, it is appropriate to have a celebration of some sort to acknowledge reaching the goal of successful communication in the target language for an entire class period.
4. As soon as learners enter the class, make sure there is a warm-up activity to complete that requires hearing, reading, writing, or interacting in the target language. The activity moves the learners from English to the target language, and serves to preview the learning for the day and/or review the learning from the prior class. You might display a photo showing a scene from the target culture with a prompt to share with a partner everything they see in the photo, or ask the learners to create a conversation as though they were in the photo.
5. Let learners determine individually when they are ready to try to use the target language for a whole class period. Learners pick up a nametag or badge when they enter class to indicate they are committed to staying in the target language 100% of the time for the class period. At the end of class everyone who has successfully stayed in the target language is acknowledged: often teachers ask students to sign a language pledge, or their name might be added to a "Language Star" poster, or the class might acknowledge them with "Bravo" or a similar exclamation.

Now let's examine teaching strategies to facilitate staying in the target language recommended by ACTFL in the position statement:

1. Provide comprehensible input that is directed toward communicative goals.

2. Make meaning clear through body language, gestures, and visual support.
3. Conduct comprehension checks to ensure understanding.

Comprehensible input is language that can be understood by learners, even when they don't understand all the grammatical structures or vocabulary in the message. Stephen Krashen (1982) described this idea in his Input Hypothesis: Learners acquire language by understanding language that is slightly beyond the learner's current level of competence. He called this (*i* + 1). Krashen (1988) states that a focus on comprehensible input helps learners acquire language naturally:

> "The best methods are therefore those that supply 'comprehensible input' in low anxiety situations, containing messages that students really want to hear. These methods do not force early production in the second language, but allow students to produce when they are 'ready', recognizing that improvement comes from supplying communicative and comprehensible input, and not from forcing and correcting production."

Placing the message in a meaningful and interesting context is a critical first step in making a message comprehensible. Interesting stories set in the target culture are excellent ways to create context. Supporting the story with photos, pictures, or a video clip helps learners understand the target language. Some instructors use costumes and props and become actors in the story, inviting learners to help them act out the storyline. Actions, gestures, emotions, facial expressions, props, drawings, photos, images, all help learners understand the message.

To ensure understanding and reassure learners that they understand what is being said, frequent comprehension checks need to be integrated throughout the lesson. These checks can be quickly accomplished with signals like "thumbs up, thumbs down" to indicate understanding, pointing to different props when they hear them said, placing pictures in the order of the story, or asking simple "yes/no" and "either/or" questions to verify understanding. As learners increase their abilities to produce language, the instructor might ask them to turn and tell a classmate the main idea of the message or retell the story that was presented, or ask their classmate simple questions modeled after ones the instructor asked.

Here are two more strategies recommended by ACTFL in the position statement:

4. Negotiate meaning with students, and encourage negotiation among students.
5. Teach students strategies for requesting clarification and assistance when faced with comprehension difficulties.

Teaching learners how to ask for clarification when they are confused or don't understand some aspect of the lesson is fundamental to survival, both in class and in places where the target language is spoken. Posting clarification questions and phrases in the target language (Figure 5) on the walls of the classroom or in a format that learners can carry in their book or notebook are great reminders for learners.

Figure 5. Clarification questions and phrases to post in classroom

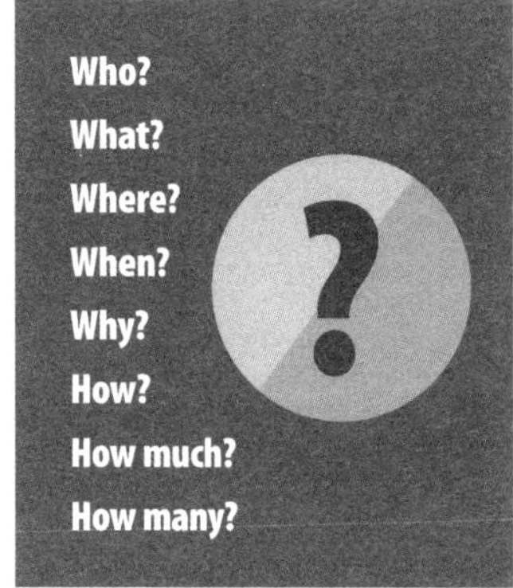

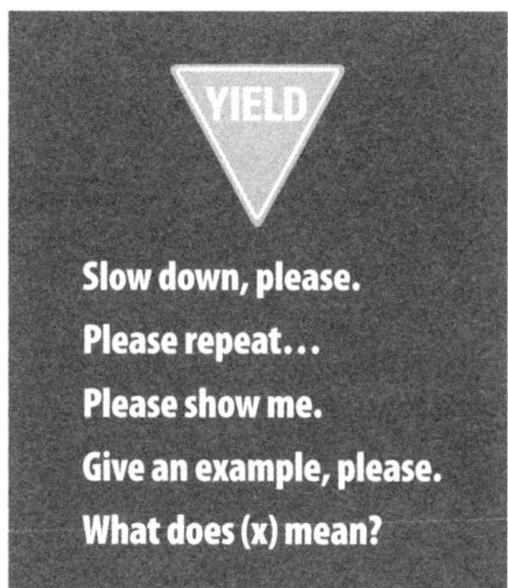

Negotiation of meaning is the process speakers go through to reach a clear understanding of each other's messages. To verify their understanding, learners might use the phrases in Figure 6:

Figure 6. Phrases to verify understanding

Negotiation of meaning and requests for clarification are real-world skills that allow learners to stay in the target language to express and to verify their understanding of what other people say.

The final strategies recommended by ACTFL in the position paper on the use of the target language in the classroom are:

6. Elicit talk that increases in fluency, accuracy, and complexity over time.
7. Encourage self-expression and spontaneous use of language.
8. Offer feedback to assist and improve students' ability to interact orally in the target language.

These last three strategies focus especially on the Interpersonal Mode: *Learners interact and negotiate meaning in spoken, signed, or written conversations to share information, reactions, feelings, and opinions.* Table 3 shows the Can-Do Performance Indicators for one function in the Interpersonal Mode, describing how learners increase their ability to express themselves spontaneously from the Novice-Low to the Intermediate-High level in two-way interactions in person or virtually. The chart of Can-Do Proficiency Benchmarks, including Advanced, Superior, and Distinguished Levels, can be found in Appendix B (ACTFL, 2017). Sample Can-Do statements for each mode of communication and for each proficiency level are also included at the website.

While small group and pair work are regularly integrated into daily lessons and units, it is equally important to connect with native speakers around the world via technology. These virtual connections are part of real-world communication and take place both formally in work situations and informally as people connect to share common interests. Learners move from scaffolded practice with their classmates to actual exchanges of ideas with native speakers. Beginning in elementary school, classrooms are connecting around the world through programs such as The Global Classroom Project (TheGlobalClassroomProject.org), iEARN (iEarn.org), One World Classrooms (OneWorldClassrooms.org), Connect All Schools (ConnectAllSchools.org), and Skype in the Classroom (https://education.microsoft.com/skypeintheclassroom). Below is one example of a sequence of steps that a Skype classroom connection could follow:

Connecting Classrooms via Skype
(Based on ideas from GloballyConnectedLearning.com)

- Select a partner school and class through Skype in the Classroom.
- Locate the school/city on a map; consult Google Earth and Google Maps.
- Decide what information you want to share with your partner class to help them get to know you and your school or community.
- Practice follow-up questions to learn more about your partner class. Create the questions you want to ask about the unit theme/topic you are exploring in class, avoiding yes/no questions.
- Organize the information you already know about the unit theme/topic and how you might share it with your partner class.
- Decide which class members will ask the questions you have prepared, and which class members will respond to the questions your partner class prepared.
- Set a date and time to Skype with your partner class.
- Record your Skype session, and have several class members take notes on the responses to the questions your class prepared.
- Assign timekeepers to signal when five minutes remain in the Skype session to close the session and thank the partner class for participating.
- Use the information from the partner class to create an Infographic/blog/podcast/video/etc. to share beyond the classroom with the partner class and with your school and community.
- At the end of the Skype project, have all learners complete a reflection: What I learned; What surprised me; What else I want to know.

Multiple opportunities for learners to use the target language to express increasingly complex thoughts and ideas, both in person and virtually, build learners' confidence and capacity to express thoughts spontaneously on a wide variety of topics, a key characteristic of proficiency, and a key skill for active participation in today's globally connected world.

Creating a Safe Environment for Learning

The learners' ability to acquire a second language is influenced by the comfort and safety they feel in a classroom, and the strength of their relationships with their classmates and instructors. Learners need to have a sense of belonging: being accepted, valued, included, and encouraged. When learners lack social and emotional connections to learning, their instructor, their school, and their peers, then behavior issues or disengagement often result, which inevitably lead to declining achievement, and, in the worst cases, dropping out of school.

Table 3. Interpersonal Mode Can-Do Performance Indicators: How can I exchange information and ideas in conversations?

Novice Low	Novice Mid	Novice High	Intermediate Low	Intermediate Mid	Intermediate High
I can provide information by answering a few simple questions on very familiar topics, using practiced or memorized words and phrases, with the help of gestures or visuals.	I can request and provide information by asking and answering a few simple questions on very familiar and everyday topics, using a mixture of practiced or memorized words, phrases, and simple sentences.	I can request and provide information by asking and answering practiced and some original questions on familiar and everyday topics, using simple sentences most of the time.	I can request and provide information in conversations on familiar topics by creating simple sentences and asking appropriate follow-up questions.	I can exchange information in conversations on familiar topics and some researched topics, creating sentences and series of sentences and asking a variety of follow-up questions.	I can exchange information in conversations and some discussions on a variety of familiar and some concrete topics that I have researched, using connected sentences that may combine to form paragraphs and asking a variety of questions, often across various time frames.

A safe environment begins by building trust between the instructor and learners. Over the first few days of a course, plan a variety of "getting acquainted" activities for different purposes: to learn each other's names; to collect background information on the learners; to help the learners find common interests with each other; to informally assess how well the learners speak the target language; or to relax the learners through participation in a game. Consider messages of fairness, competition, and equal participation that are conveyed through these first activities you choose. These first activities have the potential to set the stage for the entire semester or year. For suggestions of "getting acquainted" activities to start the school year, see Appendix C.

The nature of instruction in a world language course emphasizes collaborative activities where pairs of learners or small groups work together to complete a task. Learners and instructors again must be in a partnership to communicate that all learners are valued members of the community and are to be treated with respect and kindness as they practice communicating in the target language. Instructors can reinforce this expectation with a simple feedback mechanism called the TALK score by Shrum & Glisan (2016). Instructors keep a list of the class members on a grid with TALK written across the top. The acronym represents:

- T = Target language (participates using the target language)
- A = Accuracy (contributions are comprehensible)
- L = Listens (actively listens to what others say, reacting respectfully)
- K = Kind (helps others when they forget a word, or need encouragement)

Instructors monitor learner participation in pair work or small group work by marking a "+," "√," or "-" in each column for each learner. TALK scores can be part of the regular classroom routine and give immediate feedback to learners on both their participation in activities and on the importance of using the target language. Learners can use TALK scores to rate themselves and other members of their group on their participation.

Krashen (1982) suggests in his Affective Filter Hypothesis that successful second language acquisition is influenced by the learner's motivation, self-confidence, and anxiety level.

Classrooms that encourage low-affective filters are those that promote low anxiety among learners, that keep learners "off the defensive" (Stevick, 1976). With a supportive atmosphere as a standard operating procedure, learners are comfortable volunteering to respond to a question, to suggest an idea, to ask others for help. Most important, they are willing to take risks trying to communicate in the target language: their pronunciation may not be exact, their grammar may not be correct, or they may use an incorrect word, but no one is going to make fun of them or criticize them because everyone is learning together.

Fostering a community of learners within the classroom is another aspect of a safe environment. When learners feel that they are all working together toward a common goal, they are more engaged in the daily classroom activities. They feel they are a part of something important. That sense of community can extend beyond the classroom to others who are learning the same language. Creating a sense of community is especially important in post-secondary language classrooms, because learners often only meet two or three times per week. Beginning language learners can connect to more advanced language learners to practice speaking the target language. Learners can tutor each other or form study groups via tech tools such as Google Hangouts. Language clubs bring language learners from a variety of classes together to participate in after-class cultural enrichment activities and to practice using the target language. Virtual connections with classrooms who are also learning the target language, and with native speakers of the target language provide more opportunities to actively use the target language for real-life purposes. All these examples contribute to the sense of community, creating a safe, supportive environment for learning.

Establishing a Well-Managed Classroom

Creating a structured, well-managed classroom offers learners comfort and familiarity. Learners know that there are behavior expectations and consequences that apply to everyone. They know that each lesson will be well-organized and purposeful. They know that there are challenging but achievable learning goals for everyone. Post secondary learners understand the importance of regular class attendance in order to ensure success. By contrast, high-stress environments created by inconsistent expectations for behavior and performance make it harder for learners to focus on the lesson and more likely that they will act out or drop out. When learners know what to expect each day in class, stress and anxiety are reduced. This is true of both the youngest learners in elementary language programs and the oldest learners found in today's university language classrooms and community colleges.

Rules and Policies: Establishing and maintaining classroom rules is one of the 41 research-based strategies for effective teaching that Robert Marzano has identified (Marzano, 2017). When learners are given a legitimate voice in decision-making and learn how to use that voice effectively, they start on the path toward becoming leaders of their own learning. A whole-class discussion at the beginning of the course empowers learners to help formulate policies and procedures that are fair to all. Some classes create a class charter, outlining responsibilities and attributes of positive classroom interactions. All learners and the instructor sign the charter and post it prominently in the classroom. Figure 7 is an example of a class charter that focuses on a positive classroom environment.

Figure 7. Sample class charter

OUR CLASS CHARTER

We each have the responsibility to:

- **Come to class with a "can-do" attitude**
- **Speak German 90%+ of the time**
- **Actively participate in all activities**
- **Cooperate with others in pair and group work**
- **Respect others and their property**
- **Make sure our actions do not harm others**
- **Treat the classroom and all materials and equipment with respect**

Post-secondary instructors may want to include both learner expectations of the instructor and instructor expectations for the learner in the class syllabus. Having a place for both parties to sign off on the content of the syllabus encourages commitment to the language learning process. Another way to establish rules and policies is to provide a simple framework for behavior expectations. Figure 8 illustrates what one world language instructor provided for all classes, referring to the framework as the *4 Ps*.

Figure 8. Classroom management example called the 4Ps

Be Prompt
Be Prepared
Be Polite
Be Proactive

At the beginning of the year, the class brainstormed the significance of the *4 Ps*, creating a list of behaviors they felt reflected the *4 Ps*. "Be Prompt" included arriving on time to class, and turning in homework and projects on time. "Be Prepared" meant bringing all materials (book, notebook, pen, pencil, etc.), and completed homework to class. It also meant getting enough sleep at night and eating breakfast (at home or school/university) in order to have the energy necessary to participate actively in class. "Be Polite" meant being attentive to what the instructor and classmates say, not interrupting when others speak, making positive suggestions to help other classmates, helping the instructor and classmates as needed, and not being distracted by electronic devices. "Be Proactive" meant using the target language continuously to maximize the opportunity to practice the language in class, and asking for help before, during, and/or after class, during office hours, or via email when confused about instructions or an assignment. It also meant asking for additional ways to practice a concept or vocabulary to improve one's individual performance. While the *4 Ps* framework was generated by the instructor, the learners generated the behaviors, taking responsibility for and personalizing the framework to create a positive learning environment for their class. The instructor posted the *4 Ps* in English and the target language on the wall of the classroom where everyone could see them, and where the instructor could quickly refer to them as needed to maintain order in class. The learners also received a copy of the *4 Ps* to keep in their notebook with the behaviors that they generated for each of the Ps, to be used as another reference point as needed.

Just as it is important for learners to know the class, school, or university rules and policies, it is equally important for them to know the consequences for lack of compliance with those rules and policies. Consequences need to be communicated to all learners when the class rules and policies are presented. Consistency is the key to success. A hierarchy of consequences when a class rule is broken might build from standing near the learner, to discussing the disrupting behavior after the class period, to involving the learner in identifying potential solutions to the behavior problem.

> IDEA-SHARING
> Establishing a classroom community that respects all learners and the instructor increases learning opportunities for everyone. The community is negatively affected by disruptive behaviors where learners act out or refuse to engage in the daily activities. Share ideas about how to minimize these disruptive behaviors, and how to handle disruptions when they occur.

Routines: Routines are another important aspect of classroom management. They help learners to be organized. Routines include how class is started each day. For example, especially for beginning language learners, a calendar where the day and date and weather are highlighted is a way to contextually teach the days of the week, the months of the year, and weather as needed. Consider sharing the local weather and the weather in a city where the target language is spoken, inviting learners to find the target language city on a world map. Learners can also keep track of the weather on a chart in the classroom and/or in their notebooks. Once again, this routine is a meaningful way to practice the weather, numbers, and dates, and to familiarize the learners with the location of places where the target language is spoken. Secondary and post-secondary instructors may want to provide a calendar that students can carry in their notebooks.

Instructors often have a ritual for opening class, such as having learners turn and greet each other, practicing a proverb or saying or short poem, singing a greeting song, or completing a call and response chant. If a routine is established to begin class, learners can eventually take over leading that routine, giving them practice speaking in front of a group. Routines such as these have the added benefit of building learners' fluency. Fluency is defined here as language that becomes "automatic," because the learners have repeated the patterns many times in a familiar context. Vocabulary and language patterns that become automatic contribute to the learners' ability to speak with fewer pauses, because they need to think about what to say and how to say it less frequently. Instructors might weave questions from the previous day's class into the opening class activity, such as, "Did you tell me yesterday that you have two sisters?"

Routines that mimic practices from places where the target language is spoken bring a real-world cultural dimension to the classroom. For example, in some cultures it is appropriate for the entire class to stand when the school principal, director, or instructor enters the classroom. In some cultures, the class stands and greets the instructor before instruction begins. Learners are assigned routine duties, such as erasing the whiteboards or blackboards, handing out and collecting assignments, texts, and supplies in other cultures. These cultural routines enhance the immersive environment of the classroom and often serve as a good way to introduce commands and courtesy expressions.

Routinely revisiting the lesson objectives at the end the class period is as important as the opening routine. Make sure there is time for reflection in a learning journal entry or a check-in with a classmate on what was learned during class. Exit tickets ask learners to respond to a series of short prompts that tell the instructor and the learner if the lesson objectives were met. A typical exit ticket (Figure 9) uses a 3-2-1 format where learners provide the indicated number of responses in each row.

Figure 9. Sample 3-2-1 Exit Tickets

3	3 differences I learned today about schools in China compared to my school
2	2 new words I learned today to describe schools
1	1 question I still have

3	3 healthy eating habits I plan to adopt
2	2 pieces of advice I plan to give my family about healthy eating using the expression "You should..."
1	1 example of healthy eating habits in Italy

Exit tickets can be adapted to a variety of formats. As learners exit the classroom, they might leave Post-it notes on the classroom door with an example of a new pattern they practiced in class. Plickers.com allows instructors to check how well learners understood the key concepts of the day's lesson. If your school/univeristy has a Bring Your Own Device (BYOD) policy, learners can use text messaging to respond to question prompts with apps like PollEverywhere.com or getKahoot.com.

Other important routines that build confidence among learners include designating a time and place to hand in assignments, and a place where learners can pick up assignments and handouts from days when they were absent. Establish a routine that outlines how learners can find out what they missed when they were absent, and where they can find extra practice or help understanding new concepts. Instructors also need a routine that lets learners know where and when they are available for individual help. University instructors should post and keep regular office hours. Some instructors have more advanced learners sign up on a schedule to be available as tutors in the school library, residence halls, cafeteria, or online. If there is a designated spot for these tutors, all learners know where to go for help. Many of these routines can be incorporated into a class website or class-management system, along with a variety of resources, to reinforce and extend learning of the target language and related cultures. If a class website is not available, consider designating a bulletin board in the classroom or in a hallway near the classroom as a sort of "Help Desk" where learners can find this information.

Creating a 'Cognitively Busy' Classroom

The final element in creating a positive classroom atmosphere is what Charlotte Danielson (2013) describes as a "cognitively busy place" where learners are "intellectually active in learning important and challenging content, developing their understanding through what they do." This "cognitively busy place" is reflective of carefully planned learner-centered lessons.

When learners arrive in class, they complete an activity using the target language to set the context for the day's lesson and to transition the learners from English to the target language. The instructor may process that opening activity with the entire class to determine the learners' level of background knowledge, and to connect that knowledge to the day's lesson. Next, the instructor models new concepts and language, and then practices the new concepts and language with the class, checking for understanding during the practice. After that, the learners complete an activity using the new concepts and language in pairs or small groups with the instructor monitoring the learners' performance. Finally, learners complete a learning check individually to show both the learners and the instructor how well they understand and can use the new concept or language.

The daily activities are not mindless drills but, instead, are meaningful ways to practice the target language. Relevance and critical thinking are just as important to the design of these daily lessons as they are to the overall unit. In a cognitively busy classroom, learners are actively engaged using the world language to explore themes and topics that expand the learners' communication skills and understanding of the people and places where the target language is spoken.

Summary: As the title of this chapter indicates, a key to successfully learning a world language is to immerse the learners in a language- and culture-rich, safe learning environment. Working together, instructors and learners create a positive atmosphere for learning by following the guidelines and policies established to make classes run efficiently and effectively. The world language classroom is often noisy, as learners use the target language continuously in pairs and small groups to cooperatively explore a variety of topics. When a sense of community is established, learners are supported in their efforts to express their ideas in the target language, they are comfortable asking the instructor and their classmates for help with concepts they don't understand, and they are willing to open their minds to different ways of understanding the world. These are the characteristics of a language- and culture-rich, safe learning environment.

Reflect on the essential question: How does the classroom environment influence language learning?

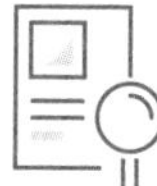

Analyze an example of a middle-school Italian class where the learners are constantly talking with each other in English.

Learners in a middle-school Italian class are all very good friends. They seem to talk non-stop in English down the hallway and into class each day. When the bell rings, the teacher has to quiet the class numerous times, and yet whispering continues as the teacher starts the lesson. The teacher has "solved" this behavior problem by giving the learners written worksheets to complete for most of the class every day. Based on this chapter, what suggestions would you give to this teacher to change the behavior of the learners?

Apply ideas to your practice using the knowledge gained from the chapter.

1. Videotape yourself and analyze the strategies you used to maintain a target language environment in the lesson. Reflect on what worked and what improvements could be made to maintain the target language by both instructor and learners.
2. Discuss rules and policies that could be adopted by the entire World Languages department to build consistency in expectations across languages and levels of instruction.

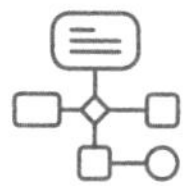

Extend your learning by completing these activities.

1. Poll your learners about strategies used in other classes to create a positive learning environment. Determine if any of them would be helpful additions to your repertoire.
2. Experiment using one of the strategies suggested in this chapter that is new for you, and reflect on its effectiveness.

Deepen your knowledge by exploring additional resources.

Target Language

Moeller, A. J., & Roberts, A. (2013). Keeping it in the target language. *CSCTFL Report 2013*. Retrieved from http://www.csctfl.org/documents/2013Report/Chapter%202.pdf

Richards, J. C. (2015). The changing face of language learning: Learning beyond the classroom. *RELC Journal*, *46*(1), 5-22.

Classroom Management

Marzano, R. J., Marzano, J. S., & Pickering, D. (2003). *Classroom management that works: Research-based strategies for every teacher.* ASCD.

Chapter 3 Communicating Effectively: Linking the Three Modes with Culture

What Kinds of Instructional Strategies Build Effective Communication?

- The Interpersonal Mode: Interacting with Clarity and Cultural Sensitivity
- The Interpretive Mode: Gaining Knowledge and Understandings About People Who Speak the Target Language
- The Presentational Mode: Presenting Ideas to Diverse Audiences Using Appropriate Media

"As my proficiency grew, I recognized that words aren't enough: understanding the integral connection between culture and language is key to being "proficient" in a language and to truly understanding others. This became even more apparent with the advent of tools such as Google Translate. Even with a lexicon composed of every word in the language, it often fails to communicate effectively because it lacks the ability to account for the degree to which cultural products, practices, and perspectives shape communication.

—Nicole Naditz, ACTFL Teacher of the Year 2015

The pathway to proficiency in more than one language is one where language and culture are intertwined throughout classroom instruction. The Communication Goal Area of the World-Readiness Standards states: "Communicate effectively in more than one language in order to function in a variety of situations and for multiple purposes" (*World-Readiness Standards for Learning Languages*, 2015). Implicit in this statement is that language alone is not sufficient. The learner must be able to function—communicate respectfully and knowledgeably—in a variety of situations and cultural contexts for a variety of purposes. The Goal Area of Cultures is integral to successful interactions in the target language, as stated in the Cultures Goal Area: "Interact with cultural competence and understanding" (*World-Readiness Standards for Learning Languages*, 2015). Moeller (2014) states: "When intercultural competence is an integral part of the language classroom, learners experience how to appropriately use language to build relationships and understandings with members of other cultures." The inextricable bond between language and culture is reaffirmed.

The Communications Goal Area includes three Standards referred to as the Modes of Communication. The Modes are: Interpersonal (Interacting in Spoken, Written, or Signed Conversations), Interpretive (Listening, Reading, Viewing), Presentational (Speaking and Writing for an Audience). While this chapter separates the three modes for the purpose of identifying strategies that are uniquely suited for each mode, it is essential to remember how the three modes support each other to build strong communication skills in the target language. Similar to the recommendation to include all major food groups in a diet to be healthy, integrating practice in all three modes is necessary to communicate successfully. The Interpersonal Mode is often used to share what has been learned individually and collectively as learners discuss their responses to the unit's essential question. The Interpretive Mode is the foundation for communication in the Presentational and Interpersonal Modes, providing information from and about the target cultures. The Presentational Mode gives space for the learners to work with the information they have learned in order to share it in original ways with an audience.

This brief overview is not meant to imply that the modes of communication are presented in a linear fashion during a unit of instruction. Quite the opposite, the modes are constantly intertwined throughout a unit of instruction, and on most days, learners practice all three Modes of Communication. Communication skills are strengthened just as a rope is strengthened when all the threads of the rope or, in this case, the three modes are interwoven. Each mode has a unique purpose in strengthening communication skills:

- The Interpersonal Mode provides the opportunity for learners to use the language and content that they have learned to spontaneously share information and ideas about the unit topic.
- The Interpretive Mode provides the model of accurate target language and the cultural content and context.
- The Presentational Mode provides the forum for learners to focus on accuracy by drafting their spoken or written message, receiving feedback from peers and the instructor on both content and language, and revising their drafts to create a polished final product for an audience.

As you read the suggested strategies for each Mode of Communication, keep in mind how the other two modes could be intertwined to strengthen communication across all modes.

The Interpersonal Mode: Interacting with Clarity and Cultural Sensitivity

Interpersonal Mode: "Learners interact and negotiate meaning in spoken, signed, or written conversations to share information, reactions, feelings, and opinions."

The Interpersonal Mode gives a glimpse of how learners will be able to communicate in real-world situations when the learners have to think on their feet. They cannot rely on a script or notes or a memorized dialogue. They have to listen carefully in order to be ready to react to what other people say. However, unlike proficiency interviews where the learner is expected to talk on a variety of unrehearsed topics, in a classroom situation, learners are exchanging information related to the unit

Table 4. Characteristics of the Interpersonal Mode

Interpersonal Communication	
Is Not	**Is**
One-way communication	Two-way communication
Face-to-face interactions exclusively	Face-to-face, cellphones, texting, email, Skype, etc., when responses, reactions are expected
Memorized	Spontaneous
Strict turn-taking	Negotiated: reacting to what others say with follow-up comments and questions
Tuning out to what others are saying	Actively listening; indicating interest with body language, eye contact
Waiting for a chance to say something which may or may not be related to the current discussion	Agreeing or politely disagreeing with various comments in the discussion; inviting others to react to what is being discussed
Overly concerned with accuracy	Focusing on understanding and being understood
Giving up and withdrawing from the interaction if you don't understand	Asking for clarification, repetition if you don't understand
Using English occasionally	Staying in the target language continuously

theme they have been studying. Table 4 displays the characteristics of the Interpersonal Mode.

Interpersonal Communication involves both listening and speaking collaboratively (Lynch, 1998). The two most important features of the Interpersonal mode are spontaneity and negotiation of meaning. Learners need to be able to begin, carry through, and end a conversation without following a memorized script. They must have a repertoire of expressions they can draw on when they don't understand what is being said or when they need clarification, all with the intention of keeping the conversation moving forward in the target language. See Figure 6 (page 17) for questions and expressions to ask for clarification.

The ACTFL Performance Descriptors (2015) outline characteristics of Interpersonal Communication at the Novice, Intermediate, and Advanced levels. Table 5 highlights the parameters of performance: Function, Content/Context, and Text Type.

Interpersonal communication on the surface is simple: it involves two or more people exchanging information, ideas, or opinions. However, the ACTFL Performance Descriptors also include Qualities of Performance: Language Control, Vocabulary, Communication Strategies, and Cultural Awareness. Cultural Awareness is an important aspect of successful communication. It includes using culturally appropriate gestures, vocabulary, and expressions, and recognizing and conforming to differences that exist in cultural behaviors. These criteria are

Table 5. Interpersonal Performance Descriptors: Parameters of Performance

Interpersonal Mode			
Domain	**Novice**	**Intermediate**	**Advanced**
Overview	Expresses self in conversations on very familiar topics using a variety of words, phrases, simple sentences, and questions that have been highly practiced and memorized.	Expresses self and participates in conversations on familiar topics using sentences and series of sentences. Handles short social interactions in everyday situations by asking and answering a variety of questions. Can communicate about self, others, and everyday life.	Expresses self fully to maintain conversations on familiar topics and new concrete social, academic, and work-related topics. Can communicate in paragraph-length conversation about events with detail and organization. Confidently handles situations with an unexpected complication. Shares point of view in discussions.
Functions	Can ask highly predictable and formulaic questions and respond to such questions by listing, naming, and identifying. May show emerging evidence of the ability to engage in simple conversation.	Can communicate by understanding and creating personal meaning. Can understand, ask, and answer a variety of questions. Consistently able to initiate, maintain, and end a conversation to satisfy basic needs and/or to handle a simple transaction. May show emerging evidence of the ability to communicate about more than the "here and now."	Can communicate with ease and confidence by understanding and producing narrations and descriptions in all major time frames and deal efficiently with a situation with an unexpected turn of events. May show emerging evidence of the ability to participate in discussions about issues beyond the concrete.
Contexts/Content	Able to function in some personally relevant contexts on topics that relate to basic biographical information. May show emerging evidence of the ability to communicate in highly practiced contexts related to oneself and one's immediate environment.	Able to communicate in contexts relevant to oneself and others, and one's immediate environment. May show emerging evidence of the ability to communicate in contexts of occasionally unfamiliar topics.	Functions fully and effectively in contexts both personal and general. Content areas include topics of personal and general interest (community, national, and international events) as well as work-related topics and areas of special competence. May show emerging evidence of the ability to communicate in more abstract content areas.
Text Type	Understands and produces highly practiced words and phrases and an occasional sentence. Able to ask formulaic or memorized questions.	Able to understand and produce discrete sentences, strings of sentences, and some connected sentences. Able to ask questions to initiate and sustain conversations.	Able to understand and produce discourse in full oral paragraphs that are organized, cohesive, and detailed. Able to ask questions to probe beyond basic details.

ACTFL Performance Descriptors (2015)

especially challenging in the context of a classroom where learners are interacting with other learners. One way to draw learners' attention to these cultural aspects of communication begins with the Interpretive Mode, where learners view video clips in a variety of cultural contexts, noting culturally appropriate gestures, vocabulary, expressions, and behaviors. Next, they create short skits integrating what they observed. Finally, the instructor asks the learners to use their interpersonal skills in unrehearsed simulations and role-plays that are similar to the video clips. Another suggestion is to draw learners' attention to culturally appropriate gestures, vocabulary, and expressions they can include in conversations. Finally, connecting with native speakers face-to-face or virtually provides another opportunity for learners to notice culturally appropriate gestures, vocabulary, and expressions, and integrate them into their interactions.

STRATEGY: Empowering learners to ask questions

The ability to ask and respond to a wide variety of questions is a basic skill that all learners need from the very first days of learning a language. As the Performance Descriptors state, Novice learners are "able to ask formulaic or memorized questions," Intermediate learners are "able to ask questions to initiate and sustain conversations," and Advanced learners are "able to ask questions to probe beyond basic details." Keeping this progression in mind reminds instructors of their roles as facilitators of classroom interactions, not leaders asking all the questions. It is helpful to share a hierarchy of questions with learners to help them ask a variety of questions. The hierarchy can be posted on a wall in the classroom in the target language as a reminder/reference for the learners. Figure 10 is a sample poster showing a hierarchy of questions.

Figure 10. Poster of a hierarchy of questions

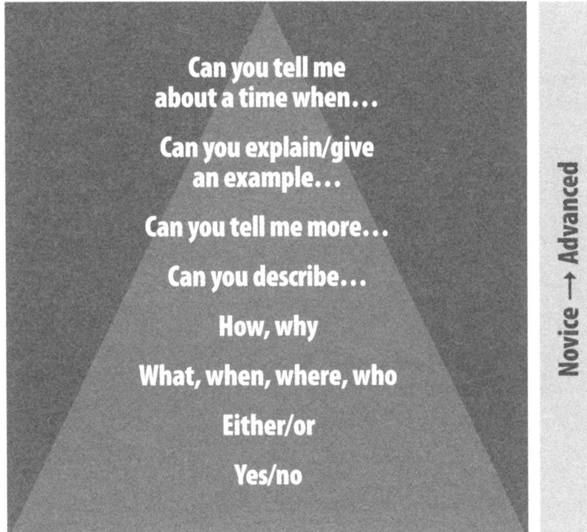

STRATEGY: Building conversation skills

Carrying on a spontaneous conversation in the target language takes practice. In a world dominated by text messages and Twitter, some contend that the art of conversation has been lost. A scaffolded approach is especially helpful for Novice language learners. It enables them to observe conversations and then try to create their own conversations based on the model. Finally, they exchange ideas and information spontaneously without planning or rehearsal. The process may be revisited with Intermediate language learners to demonstrate and practice how to maintain a conversation with extended comments and reactions.

- **Step 1.** Modeling – Learners watch a video clip or a role play of a conversation that includes questions, responses, and reactions. They debrief the kinds of questions, responses, and reactions they observed.
- **Step 2.** Scripts – Give learners a similar situation to the modeled conversation, and have them work in pairs or small groups to create a conversation that includes questions, responses, and reactions. Learners practice the conversation they have created.
- **Step 3.** Cues – Give learners a situation and have them work in pairs to create a list of key words or phrases that cue the kinds of questions, reactions, and comments they might incorporate to maintain a conversation. They should not write a full script. Learners practice the conversation based on the cues they listed.
- **Step 4.** Situations – Give learners a situation similar to the ones practiced in Steps 2 and 3. Ask the learners to interact in the situation without the benefit of scripts, notes, or rehearsal.

STRATEGY: Creating a real need to exchange information

Real communication takes place when one person has information that another person wants or needs. Known as information gap activities, they are most engaging when the learners need missing information to complete a task or project. For example, learners are completing an authentic information gap activity when they compare lists of props needed for a skit and then find out which props each group member can contribute to the staging of the skit. In another example, learners survey classmates to find out favorite songs or films in order to create an infographic to share with a class in a country where the target language is spoken.

Another way to create a real need to exchange information is to give individual learners or groups responsibility for different topics related to the unit theme. They need to research their topic and then share their information with others with the goal of broadening everyone's knowledge base.

Sometimes exchanging information is structured around a text that is broken into segments in a jigsaw activity. The class is divided into groups. Each group is given a segment of the text to read and discuss. Then new groups are formed, composed of representatives from each of the original groups. The members of the new groups share the key ideas from the segments of the text they read. In turn, they receive key information about the segments they didn't read, in order to have a complete summary of the text. The real need for information others have is created and achieved through these types of activities.

STRATEGY: Creating real-world contexts for spontaneous interactions

Board games from the target cultures create situations in the classroom where learners can use the target language spontaneously as they play the game. Many board games from around the world with playing rules are available online. One such site is https://nrich.maths.org/8261 which includes the countries of origin, diagrams for the game boards, and simple instructions. Other sites include downloadable boards that can be copied for use in class. Using authentic games from the target cultures immerses learners in both language and culture as they play.

Introducing a new game to learners includes simplifying and printing out the rules for the game to discuss before play begins. It is helpful to create a vocabulary list of the parts of the game (game board, dice, spinner, marker, spaces on the board) and a list of expressions that facilitates using the target language to play the game. Examples include: It's your turn; Who is next? Roll the dice; Move forward/backward (x) spaces. Make the games available for learners to use in the classroom, to check out in order to play them during free time in an activity area, outdoors, or to take home or to a residence hall to play with their families and friends.

STRATEGY: Building natural interactions

To help learners sound more "natural" in their interactions, teach and post a list of reactions that they can incorporate as they speak. Figure 11 includes some suggestions for these reactions.

Figure 11. Poster of suggested reactions

STRATEGY: Managing Successful Group Discussions

Group discussions facilitate interpersonal communication as the learners contribute and react spontaneously to what others say. Instructors can organize group discussions in a variety of ways to strengthen the learners' abilities to actively participate in a discussion.

- **Assigned discussion leader:** The leader sets the stage for the discussion by reviewing the topic, adding a new perspective to the topic, or posing questions to move the discussion forward. The discussion leader also monitors the discussion to ensure that everyone is given the opportunity to speak, to keep the discussion on track, and to maintain a respectful exchange of ideas.
- **Clusters:** To encourage all learners to participate, especially when group discussion is a new strategy, it helps to break groups into subgroups or clusters as a first step. In groups of three or four, learners discuss the topic or questions for a few minutes, recalling potential content and vocabulary needed for active participation. Then two clusters come together to form a group and share with each other what they discussed. The "rehearsal stage" in clusters gives all learners a chance to practice how they might actively contribute to the larger group discussion.
- **Think/Pair/Share:** As a homework assignment, learners complete a graphic organizer in response to a question that will be discussed in groups. In class, learners pair with someone to share their ideas. Next, the pair joins with one or two other pairs to share their ideas in a small group

discussion. The graphic organizer serves as a reminder of their ideas in the form of key words and phrases.

- **Note-taking Synthesis:** As a follow-up to an assignment where learners had to take notes on a reading, a presentation, or a video clip, the learners work in groups of four to compare the notes they took, in order to create a "master" synthesis of the most important ideas. This helps all learners review the text, identify the key ideas, and create a summary that can be used to prepare for a group discussion on the unit topic.
- **Chain Reaction:** Groups of six to eight learners respond to a question or idea, moving in order from one learner to the next, going around the discussion circle. Each learner must add to the discussion by expanding on what someone else said. The focus of this activity is on listening to what others say, and building on their ideas to create a cohesive discussion.
- **Scored Discussion:** Groups are set up in a fishbowl configuration, half of the learners facing each other in an inner circle, half of the learners positioned around the inner circle in an outer circle. The inner circle group discusses a topic or question or text. Each person in the outer circle is assigned to observe one person in the inner circle to evaluate his or her participation. Table 6 shows a sample evaluation form that the observers can use to assess the participants' contributions to the discussion. The discussion might be as short as 5 minutes or as long as 15 minutes. At the end of the discussion, the observers meet individually for three minutes with the people they observed to share their observations. At the end of this debriefing, the groups switch, with the observers moving to the inner circle and the inner circle learners moving to the outer circle as observers. The topic/questions may change or remain the same depending on the goals for the discussion. The discussion now begins again with the new inner circle participants. At the end of the time period, the observers debrief with the people they observed. The debriefing may be followed by a full class debriefing/discussion of the topic.

Table 6. Evaluation of participation in scored discussion

	Yes	No
Stays in the target language		
Initiates an idea to be discussed		
Adds related information to continue the discussion		
Monitors personal contributions; does not dominate the discussion		
Expresses personal opinion about the topic with justification		
Asks questions related to the topic		
Responds to questions with explanations		
Brings group back to the topic when discussion moves off topic		
Asks for input from a person who has not contributed to the discussion		
Listens attentively to others		
Strengths in participation:		
Suggestion to improve participation:		

STRATEGY: Building Interpersonal Writing

Interpersonal communication can take place in written form when the message is created spontaneously with the expectation of a response. Learners can exchange messages with classmates and the instructor using a website such as Edmodo.com. They can share ideas, ask, and respond to questions similar to exchanges that take place on Facebook and other social networks. If there are barriers to communicating through technology, learners can "simulate" sending text messages by posting short messages on a whiteboard in the classroom. Another "low tech" possibility is for learners to write a message to an assigned partner, place the message in an envelope, and place it in a class mailbox. The envelopes are distributed as part of the opening of the class or as a concluding activity. Learners read their messages and respond to them, returning the envelope with the response to the mailbox to be opened during the next class period.

The Importance of the Interpersonal Mode: The Interpersonal Mode gives learners the opportunity to interact with others without scripting what they will say. Frequent interactions in these unrehearsed situations builds confidence in the learners that they can understand and use the target language in real-world situations outside the classroom. ***Additional activities to build Interpersonal communication skills are located in Appendix D.***

> IDEA-SHARING
> Providing timely feedback to learners helps them improve their performance. How do you make sure learners receive feedback as they practice their interpersonal skills in pair work and small group work?

The Interpretive Mode: Gaining Knowledge and Understandings About People Who Speak the Target Language

Interpretive Mode: Learners understand, interpret, and analyze what is heard, read, or viewed on a variety of topics.
(*World-Readiness Standards for Learning Languages*, 2015)

Through reading, listening, and viewing, learners build their knowledge and understanding of a wide variety of topics that they can share with others through the Presentational and Interpersonal Modes. For learners to produce the target language with attention to accuracy, vocabulary, and cultural awareness, they need to have real-world examples of oral, visual, and written authentic texts. Authentic texts are those texts created by native speakers for native speakers (Shrum & Glisan, 2016), with "texts" including those that are oral, written, and visual. Authentic texts model how native speakers create messages in the target language. They are language- and culture-rich in the way the genre is represented, in the choice of topic and vocabulary, in the syntax, the format and organization of the text, and in the choice of illustrations and images. Think of an authentic text as a sort of native speaker in the classroom, modeling correct language and sharing cultural perspectives with the learners.

Demonstrating understanding of written, spoken, and visual texts in the Interpretive Mode means that, at times, learners use English (L1) to explain what they understood. That said, instructors need to control the use of English, and move the discussion of texts into the target language as appropriate for the language levels of the learners and the required complexity of response. Research supports the use of L1 to check understanding in the Interpretive Mode, especially for Novice language learners, because they can explain in greater depth what they understand when they are not limited by what they can express in the target language (Shrum & Glisan, 2016).

Let's consider the characteristics of the Interpretive Mode presented in Table 7.

Table 7. Characteristics of the Interpretive Mode

Interpretive Communication	
Is Not	**Is**
Two-way interaction to clarify meaning	One-way communication
Written texts only	Written, audio, visual texts
Culture-neutral	Culture-rich
Word-for-word translation	Understanding the main idea and supporting details
Identification of all information, including trivial details	Identification of information and details needed to accomplish the purpose for reading, listening, viewing
Dependence on a dictionary	Using context to make logical guesses about the meaning of new vocabulary

The learners are receivers of information in the Interpretive Mode, with no opportunity to ask for clarification or explanation unless the situation is adjusted to accommodate follow-up questions and clarifications. For example, at the end of listening to a speech or watching a film or reading a novel, there may be an opportunity to move to the Interpersonal Mode for a group discussion or Question-and-Answer about the text. Notice that, when receiving messages, if the learner interacts with others about the message, the mode changes. Taking this example one step further, after taking in a message (Interpretive Mode) and discussing the message with others (Interpersonal Mode), the learners might use the information and insights gained from the Interpretive and Interpersonal Modes to prepare a report or critical review (Presentational Mode). Micken (2013) states: "Text encounters are opportunities for action—for expression of points of view, for argument, for dispute—and for negotiation, agreement, affirmation, and confirmation" (p. 39). This quote underlines the interrelationship among the three modes. While the Interpretive Mode is about receiving messages, the learners then have to do something with what they learned from the message: they can share their learning with others (Interpersonal Mode) and/or they can use what they learned to prepare oral and written presentations for a variety of audiences and purposes (Presentational Mode). This illustrates how the modes are interrelated and interdependent, supporting each other to complete a full circle of communication.

The ACTFL Performance Descriptors (2015) provide characteristics of the types of texts that learners can understand at the Novice, Intermediate, and Advanced levels. Table 8 describes what learners can understand in terms of Function, Content/Context, and Text Type at the Novice, Intermediate, and Advanced levels.

Note that performance at the Novice level is based on understanding texts "with highly predictable, familiar contexts." Prior knowledge related to the topic and vocabulary, along with visual support, are also critical to understanding. The availability of authentic texts is almost endless, given the access that the Internet provides to resources from around the world. Keeping in mind learners' age, language level, and prior

Table 8. Interpretive Performance Descriptors: Parameters of Performance

Interpretive Mode			
Domain	**Novice**	**Intermediate**	**Advanced**
Overview	Understands words, phrases, formulaic language that have been practiced and memorized to get meaning of the main idea of simple, highly predictable oral and written texts with strong visual support.	Understands the main idea and some supporting details on familiar topics in a variety of texts.	Understands main ideas and supporting details on familiar and some new, concrete topics from a variety of more complex texts that have a clear organized structure.
Functions	Comprehends meaning through recognition of key words and formulaic phrases that are highly contextualized. May show emerging evidence of the ability to make inferences based on background and prior knowledge.	Comprehends main ideas and identifies some supporting details. May show emerging evidence of the ability to make inferences by identifying key details from the text.	Comprehends the main idea and supporting details of narrative, descriptive, and straightforward persuasive texts. Makes inferences and derives meaning from context and linguistic features.
Contexts/Content	Comprehends texts with highly predictable, familiar contexts (those related to personal background, prior knowledge, or experiences.)	Comprehends information related to basic personal and social needs, and relevant to one's immediate environment such as self and everyday life, school, community, and particular interests.	Comprehends texts pertaining to real-world topics of general interest relevant to personal, social, work-related, community, national, and international contexts.
Text Type	Derives meaning when authentic texts (listening, reading, or viewing) are supported by visuals or when the topic is very familiar. Comprehends texts ranging in length from lists, to phrases, to simple sentences, often with graphically organized information.	Comprehends simple stories, routine correspondence, short descriptive texts or other selections within familiar contexts. Generally comprehends connected sentences and much paragraph-like discourse. Comprehends information-rich texts with highly predictable order.	Comprehends paragraph discourse such as that found in stories, straightforward literary works, personal and work-related correspondence, written reports or instructions, oral presentations, news, anecdotes, descriptive texts, and other texts dealing with topics of a concrete nature.

knowledge about a topic and related vocabulary helps instructors select articles, stories, video-clips, etc. that are appropriate for the learners. It isn't until the Advanced level that learners are expected to understand topics unfamiliar to them.

Instructors who navigate the Internet using browsers from countries where the target language is spoken will find authentic texts that may not appear on U.S.-based search engines. For example, Yahoo International (http://everything.yahoo.com/world/) links to many different versions of Yahoo around the world. It is also helpful to search using key phrases and vocabulary in the target language associated with a topic. For example, to develop an instructional unit based on the question: "What if all the trees disappear?," instructors might search for forests, deforestation, reforestation, urban green spaces, trees as symbols, trees in literature, etc.

Think creatively to seek out new sources for authentic texts. Several National Foreign Language Resource Centers (NFLRC), universities, and professional language organizations have begun collections of authentic resources for classroom use. Many individual instructors are also sharing resources they have found via websites, blogs, and Pinterest.

Another way to find authentic texts is to connect with classroom instructors in countries where the target language is spoken and ask them what their students are reading, listening to, or viewing for both academic purposes and for personal enrichment and enjoyment. There are several services that connect classrooms around the world. Examples are listed on page 18 of Chapter 2 of this publication.

Building a classroom library of authentic oral, written, and visual texts is also important. Providing "hands on" access within the classroom is a great way to encourage learners to explore topics of personal interest independently. Multiple opportunities to read, listen to, and view a wide variety of authentic texts develops proficiency, vocabulary, awareness of syntax, and cultural understanding among learners (Day & Barnford, 1998).

In addition to authentic texts, semi-authentic texts and created texts also enable learners to interpret materials in the target language. Semi-authentic texts are created by native and/or non-native speakers based on authentic texts but adapted to meet curricular goals. Created texts are original texts authored by native or non-native speakers and designed specifically for non-native speakers to meet curricular goals. Semi-authentic and created texts are not replacements for authentic texts. They are, however, very useful in building a learner's abilities and confidence in interpreting texts in the target language.

Learners at all levels of proficiency benefit from interacting with authentic texts because they are real-world, they model correct language, and they reflect authentic culture. "Edit the task, not the text" (Shrum & Glisan, 2016) guides some of the decisions instructors make as they provide multiple opportunities for learners to interpret a wide variety of authentic texts. Consider these three questions when selecting authentic texts:

- Why are the learners reading/listening to/viewing this text, and what will they learn from it?
- What questions will learners need to answer?
- What will learners be able to do with the information they learn from the text?

Equally important to the instructor's purposeful selection of texts is sharing the purpose for reading, listening to, viewing a text with the learners. How we approach authentic texts is similar to how we approach texts in our native language. Sometimes we want to know only the main idea. Sometimes we are searching for specific information. Sometimes we want to know more details, so will read more intently. Sometimes the motive is simply enjoyment with no expectation of recounting details. Multiple opportunities to interact with authentic texts of all kinds strengthen learners' abilities to interpret texts. Through modeling how to approach a text and then providing support to the learners as they explore the text, learners build their capacity to unlock meaning in authentic texts.

Strategies for Listening, Reading, Viewing

The strategies in this section are useful for all types of texts—oral, written, visual—and support learners' literacy development. Strategies specifically designed for building one of the receptive skills follow this opening segment on strategies applicable to all three skills. Kate Paesani, Director of CARLA (Center for Advanced Research on Language Acquisition at the University of Minnesota), states in the September 5, 2016, issue of *InterCom*: "...communication takes place through more than written means; it entails interacting with written, audio, audiovisual, and visual information to convey messages through language. Spoken language is thus closely linked to one's ability to communicate about textual content and to being literate in a language" (Kern, 2015).

STRATEGIES: Pre-reading, Pre-listening, Pre-viewing

Pre-reading, pre-listening, pre-viewing strategies are fundamental to literacy development in all languages, helping learners make connections between a new text and what they already know about the topic. There is a strong correlation between prior knowledge and reading comprehension even if the learner's reading ability is low (Paesani, Allen, & Dupuy, 2016). Prior knowledge also facilitates listening and viewing comprehension. Here are three steps to complete in the pre-reading, pre-listening, pre-viewing phase:

Elicit background knowledge that learners may have about the topic of the text. This can be done in a variety of ways. Images related to the topic are powerful reminders of past learning and personal experiences. Asking learners to brainstorm what they see or know about the images helps not only the learners but also the instructor make connections to new learning. Remind the learners to notice the cultural context: what cultural products and practices appear in the images. Allow learners to brainstorm about the images in pairs or small groups to maximize the active participation of all learners in a class. The ideas they generate can be documented in a word cloud using Wordle (http://www.wordle.net) or Tagxedo (http://www.tagxedo.com). Figure 12 is an example of a word cloud created using Tagxedo.

Figure 12. Word Cloud using Tagxedo

Another strategy for activating learners' prior knowledge is K-W-L, a metacognition strategy developed by Donna Ogle (1986). The K-W-L chart or organizer is set up in three columns. Under the "K" column, learners write what they already **know** about the topic or theme. The information provided by learners through the "K" column gives instructors information about learners' readiness levels for the new theme, misconceptions the learners hold about it, and gaps in knowledge. In the "W" column, learners reflect on what they **want to learn** about the new topic. Ideas generated by learners in the "W" column provide information to instructors about how to better motivate and engage learners in the new learning. Educators craft subsequent lessons to address some of the ideas generated by learners in the "W" column. The "L" column, completed by learners at the end of the learning sequence, allows learners to reflect on what they have **learned**, bringing the experience full circle. The information generated by learners in the "L" column provides summative information to educators about what each learner is taking away from the unit or theme studied. Table 9 is an example of the KWL chart in English and in Spanish.

Table 9. KWL Chart in English and Spanish

K What I know	W What I want to know	L What I learned
S *Lo que sé*	*Q* *Lo que quiero saber*	*A* *Lo que aprendí*

Preview the text with the learners. Look at layout, titles, headings, bold print, photos, charts, and captions in written texts to determine which of the categories identified during brainstorming of background knowledge seem to be most relevant. If the text is audio, have the learners listen the first time for sounds that give clues to location such as the roar of the crowd, the sound of the ocean. Listen for emotions in the voices of the speakers, along with their gender and age. Listen for the style: does it sound like a newscast, a play-by-play for a sport, a dramatic presentation, an emotional conversation, etc. If the text is a video clip, watch the video the first time with the sound turned off in order to focus on the images and people in the clip, to get a sense of the context for the interactions.

As part of the preview, discuss the cultural context. If the context is familiar to the learners, they can contribute understandings from their past experiences with the context. If this is a new context, learners may pose questions or complete the sentence stem "I wonder…." Following the preview, the instructor highlights cultural details important to the understanding and appreciation of the text. The next step is to make predictions.

Predict what the text is about, using the information gleaned from the preview phase. Beginners might draw a picture of their prediction of the main idea. More advanced learners might make several suggestions about the possible content of the text. They can then determine if these predictions are true or false as they read/listen to/view the text, highlighting or noting ideas from the text that support the true statements. After completing the text, learners can correct the predictions they made that are false. In the case where the prediction is not included in the text at all, they can delete that prediction. Now it's time to gather more information from the text.

STRATEGIES: During Reading/Listening/Viewing

Learners benefit from reading/listening/viewing with a partner to help each other understand the text. After reading/listening/viewing a segment of the text, they can check their understanding with each other, show each other where they found the information requested in what they just read, listened to, or viewed. In the case of audio or video texts, and if the partners are able to replay the text, they can listen to or view segments several times if needed to clarify or verify their understanding. The following strategies help learners unlock meaning in the text:

- **Read/listen/view - then react!:** As learners read/listen to/view a text, they can pause after a segment to react to the text instead of waiting until after they have read/listened to/viewed the entire text. They might write a question that they have about the content (a clarification or a request for more information). They might react with an exclamation ("That's amazing!" "Really?") and a comment about the idea that caused that reaction. They might make an association to something earlier in the text, or to another text, or to a personal experience. They might note a big idea. All of these reactions can be written in the margin of written texts or, especially for audio or video texts, they can be added to a journal where learners keep track of the authentic texts they have explored. In their journal they identify the text, and then add their notes with their questions, reactions, associations. After completing the text, the learner's final entry might be a draft of a summary of the text, a reaction to the text, a critic's review of the text, or an outline of what they learned from the text in terms of content and also in terms of cultural understandings.
- **Visual notetaking:** As learners read/listen to/view a text, they pause periodically to draw pictures or fill in parts of a graphic organizer to represent how the ideas or information are connected. Afterward, they exchange and compare drawings or graphic organizers to see if they captured the same ideas. Learners can discuss points of disagreement on the content and/or add to their pictures or graphic organizers. After sharing their ideas, learners can individually summarize or retell the information in the text, using their visual notes. Figure 13 (see p. 36) is an example of visual notetaking with some suggestions for how to start taking notes visually.
- **Text to self, text to text, text to world:** Research shows that understanding increases when learners make connections to what they are reading (Pearson et al., 1979; King et al., 1997). In the first type of connections, as learners read, listen to, or view a text, they take notes about connections between the text and their own experiences and prior knowledge: text to self. For example, instructors can model this strategy by pausing a video clip about young people in Germany playing soccer at a public park. The instructor might say (in the target language): "This reminds me of how I spent my summers when I was growing up. We lived near a park, and there were always kids playing soccer. I loved to go there. Sometimes I watched a game, and sometimes I played. Do you ever do something like that?" Learners can respond to the question in pairs, and then share with the class. The instructor can then follow this with a question about how the action in the video clip is similar and different from the learners' experiences.

In text to text, learners compare the current text they are studying to one that they have previously read, listened to, or viewed. For example, learners might be exploring the essential question: Why do we have legends? In a Mandarin class, learners might compare the role of the dragon in various texts. They can also compare legends about the dragon to legends they know from their own experiences. Learners might also compare the structure of the legends, identifying the beginning, middle, and end of the story.

Finally, in text to world, learners compare an event they are learning about to something that is or has happened in their community or in the world. Latin classes often

Figure 13. Visual notetaking example

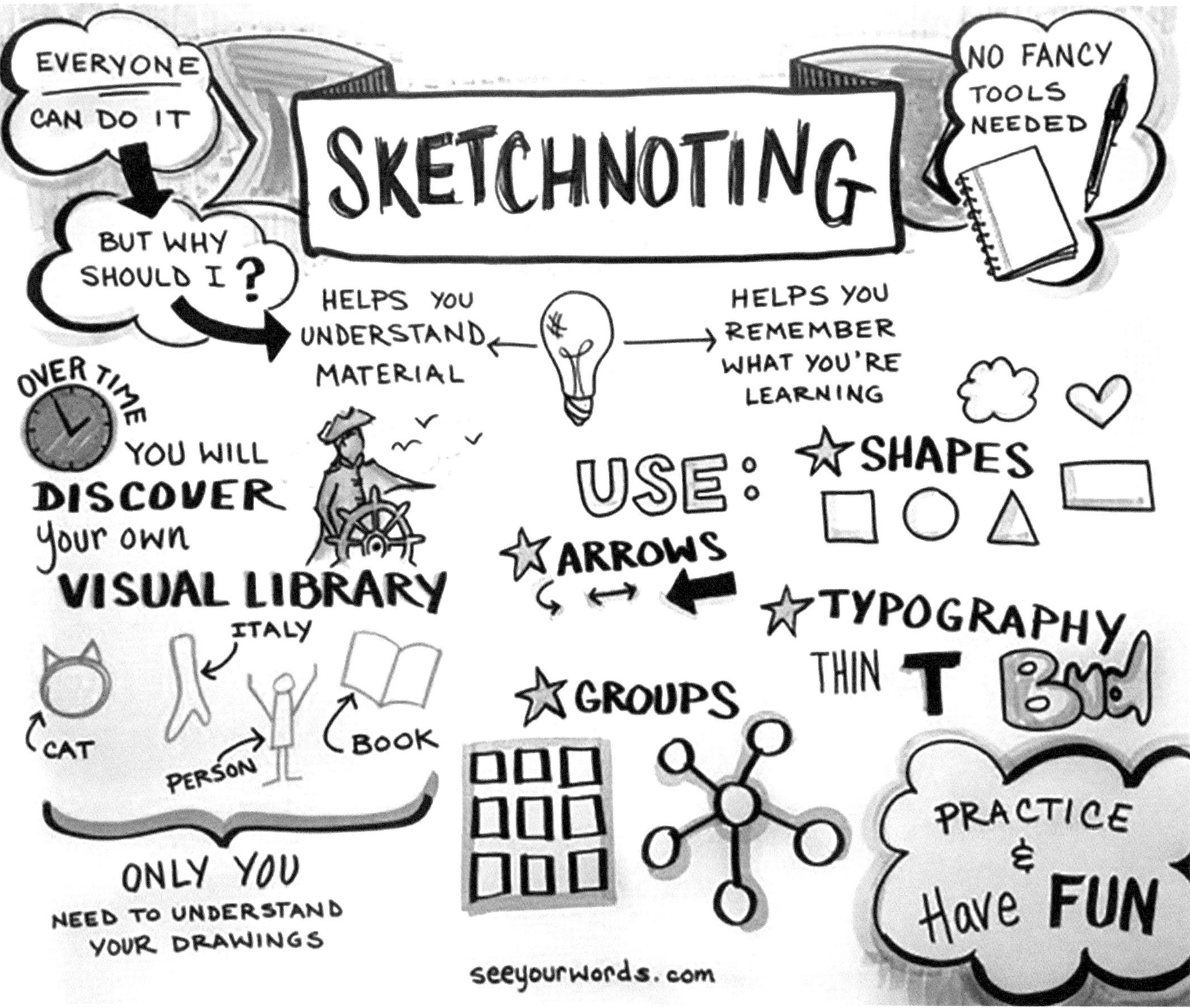

study about how Pompeii was destroyed by the eruption of Mount Vesuvius. This event from the past lends itself to comparison to natural disasters in the world today. The more connections learners can make between what they know to new texts in the target language, the easier it becomes for them to locate and understand the main ideas and supporting details.

STRATEGIES: After Reading/Listening/Viewing

After reading/listening/viewing a text, learners need to verify their understanding of the text. Here are some alternatives to answering comprehension questions.

- **Main idea and supporting details detection:** Provide learners with three to five options for the main idea of a text before they read, listen to, or view the text. After listening/reading/viewing, the learner circles the option that reflects the main idea, and justifies their option referencing components such as the title, the opening sentence of the text, images, emphasis of select ideas, etc.

Help learners connect the main idea of a text with supporting details by having them complete a graphic organizer showing the relationship between the main idea and the supporting details. A variety of graphic organizers in their completed version, and also as blank templates, can be found at: http://carla.umn.edu/cobaltt/modules/strategies/gorganizers/EDITABLE.HTML

Figure 14 is an example using the graphic organizer called **The 5 Ws + How**. As learners read the text, they note responses to Who? What? Where? When? Why? and How?

Figure 14. Internet article with graphic organizer to note main ideas

EXPONAUTE.COM

Quand le Louvre invite trois youtubeurs

Signalé par **Pierre Haski** Cofondateur. Publié le 17/02/2016 à 05h12 **7 024** VISITES

En matière de visibilité sur le Web, le Louvre a de quoi faire des envieux. Avec ses 3,6 millions d'abonnés réunis par quatorze comptes différents (Facebook, Twitter, Instagram...), le musée entend bien entériner sa présence sur le Net. Nouvelle étape depuis le début du mois de février : engager de célèbres youtubeurs, pour que ces derniers réalisent des vidéos dans les couloirs de l'institution, afin de s'adresser à un public plus jeune.

Selon le site Exponaute.com, le plus grand musée du monde a ainsi contacté trois célèbres vidéastes -- Axolot, Nota Bene et Le Fossoyeur de Films – pour leur proposer de réaliser, chacun, deux vidéos : une première à poster directement sur leur chaîne YouTube et une seconde qui sera directement diffusée sur la chaîne officielle de l'institution parisienne. Chacun des youtubeurs apporte sa « patte » et son regard original sur le Louvre et son histoire.

Article retrieved from: http://rue89.nouvelobs.com/
Original website for opensource newspapers: http://theopensourcenewspaper.org/

Quand le Louvre invite trois youtubeurs *(When the Louvre invites 3 YouTube designers)*				
Quoi? *(What?)*	**Quand?** *(When?)*	**Où?** *(Where?)*	**Qui?** *(Who?)*	**Pourquoi?** *(Why?)*
Vidéos sur le Louvre et son histoire *(Videos about the Louvre and its history)*	Depuis février 2016 *(Since February, 2016)*	Au Louvre *(At the Louvre)*	Des youtubeurs *(YouTube designers)*	Attirer les jeunes *(To attract young people)*
Idée principale: Depuis février 2016, le Louvre invite des youtubeurs au Louvre pour réaliser des vidéos sur le Louvre et son histoire pour attirer les jeunes. *(Beginning in February 2016, the Louvre has been inviting YouTube designers to make videos about the Louvre and its history in order to attract young people.)*				

- **Sequencing:** Provide learners with five or six images that reflect the text. Learners place the images in order according to the text. This can be followed by a Presentational task, where the learners write captions for the images or retell the information in the text based on the images.
- **Inferences:** Learners can begin to identify inferences in a text, even as novice learners. After reading/listening to/viewing a text such as the one above about attracting young people to the Louvre, learners can respond to questions such as: Do you think that the text is fact, or fiction? Why? Why do you think the Louvre wants to attract young people to the museum? These questions ask learners to go beyond what is printed in the article, drawing on higher-order thinking skills to justify their responses.
- **Summarizing:** Ask learners to summarize the main ideas of the text they heard/listened to/viewed. It is helpful to model summary statements for learners before asking them to create summaries. One way to model summarizing is to give learners a list of statements that were included in the text, and have them select the ones that capture the big ideas. Next have them work in pairs to organize their selected statements into a paragraph. The instructor might give them a word bank of transition words and connectors to use in their paragraph.
- **Create a title:** Ask learners to create a title for the text that they read/listened to/viewed. After creating the title, ask them to explain why they chose the title. Explaining the title is another way to help learners summarize the most important ideas from a text.

STRATEGIES: Vocabulary Recognition

There are many words we understand but do not actively use, even though we have seen or heard them in context many times. This segment focuses on passive vocabulary, those words we understand in context when we hear or read them but have not transferred to active use when we speak or write in the target language.

- **Logical Guessing from Context:** When instructors and learners take time to access background knowledge, preview, and predict the main ideas of a text, learners have a head start on using context to make logical guesses about the meanings of unknown words. Figure 15 (see p. 38) shows an example where background experience with cooking and recipes, along with the visuals, help the learner make logical guesses about the meanings of words they might be seeing for the first time in this recipe.

Figure 15. Recipe in Portuguese

- **Language-specific cues to meaning:** Here is another very effective strategy for unlocking the meaning of unknown words. Some learners seem to notice cognates and patterns automatically, while other learners do not. Instructors who model think-alouds about how they make logical guesses related to the meaning of an unknown word help learners develop those same strategies. Language-specific cues include:
  - identifying root words, prefixes, and suffixes;
  - listing related words (word families);
  - highlighting verb endings that signal time frames;
  - pointing out word order that gives clues to whether the unknown word is an action or person, place, or thing.
  - finding words that look and or sound nearly the same in the native language, and then using context to help determine if the word is a cognate or a false cognate.

Figure 16 is a graphic that shows learners what to do when they don't know a word. Enlarging this image and posting it in the classroom is a way to empower learners to take responsibility for their learning.

Figure 16. What to do when you don't know a word

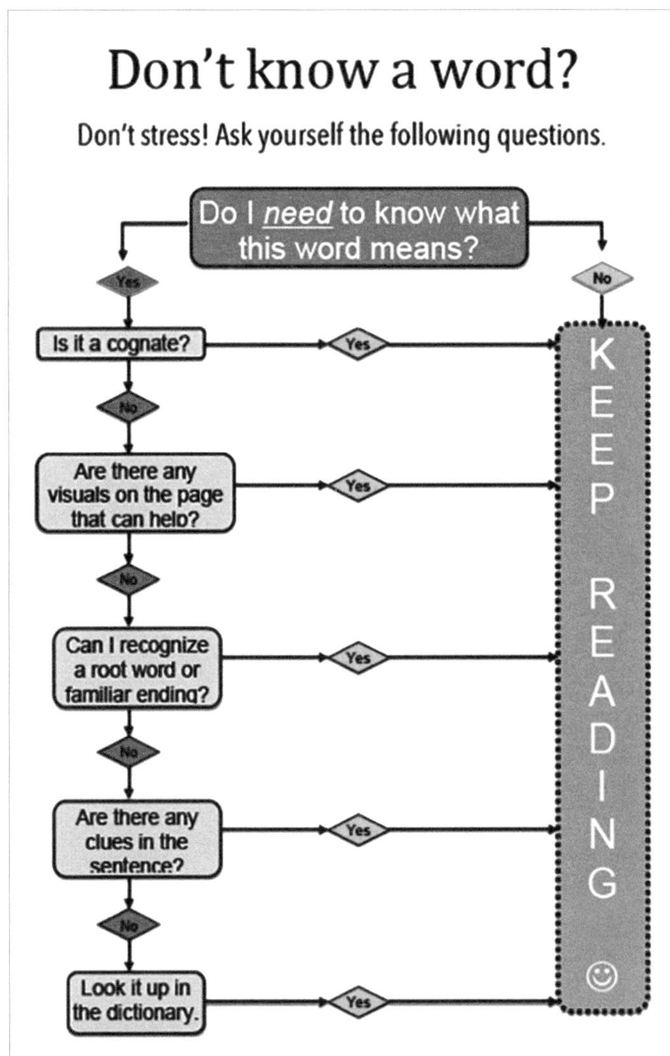

Heather Sherrow (Howard County Public Schools, MD)

Here is an example from an Italian class. Learners receive an infographic about the cinema in Italy (Figure 17). Their own experiences give them ideas about the type of information they might find in the infographic. The images help them understand the text. In this example in Italian, cognates also help learners figure out the message. While cognates seem obvious to many learners, they are not apparent to all, and do depend on how rich the learners' vocabulary is in their native language. There is also text in the infographic that is not directly connected to a visual, and does not contain cognates, for example, the box in the upper right-hand corner of the infographic: "*Arriva ovunque, è veloce è affidabile, è ecologico.*" Using the chart in Figure 16, learners can determine that they can keep on reading because the information in the box is not essential, or they can go through the steps on the left to unlock the meaning of the unknown words in the box.

It is helpful for learners to work in pairs to make logical guesses about the information on the infographic. They can help each other connect the images to the text, and make logical guesses based on the images, cognates, and language they know. At this point, you might be wondering whether the learners are using the target language or their native language to make those logical guesses. If the learners are accustomed to staying in the target language, and by extension are used to figuring out how to say what they want to say without falling into their native language, you have your answer. There will always be infrequent occasions when English may be needed for a brief explanation, but that is the exception, not the rule. Keep in mind that logical guessing should not turn into a translation exercise.

Strategies Specific to Building Listening Skills

Listening is a complex skill made especially challenging in "live" situations where learners must react very quickly to figure out the purpose for listening, and activate background knowledge about the topic. They must be able to predict or anticipate content, and attend to the parts of the message that are relevant to the identified purpose. All of these actions occur almost instantaneously as the learner is hearing the message. Researchers note a decline over the past several years in people's ability to listen carefully to others and to react to and retain the information received. Some say this is the result of multi-tasking, where people do not concentrate on a single

Figure 17. Infographic in Italian about the cinema in Italy

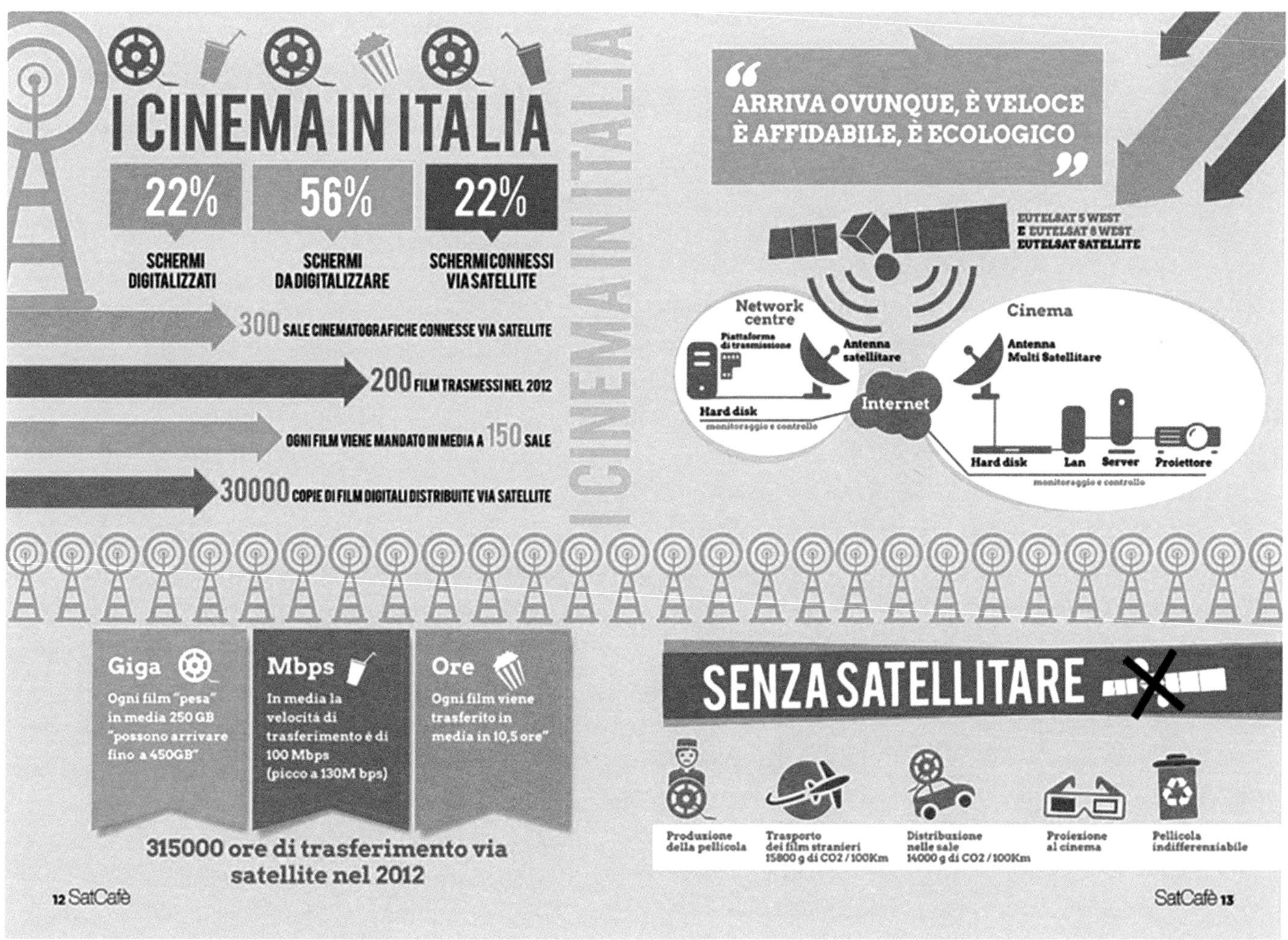

http://www.eutelsat.com/events/eutelsat-italia

message but, instead, move among several resources quickly and superficially.

Building listening skills begins the very first day of class, when the instructor introduces learners to an immersive environment by using the target language almost exclusively. Given the short amount of time learners are in a world language class, it is important to maximize the amount of comprehensible target language the learners hear (see Chapter 2 for a complete discussion on the use of the target language in the world language classroom). Taking time to give tips to learners on how to listen heightens their awareness of how to process incoming messages. Instructors working with young learners often remind them to listen not only with their ears, but also with their eyes, mouths, and hands. Listening with your eyes means being observant: look at the visuals and props, pay attention to gestures and facial expressions, and watch the instructor's mouth for pronunciation cues. Listening with mouths means refraining from talking when others are talking in order to hear what is being said. Listening with hands means that learners have to avoid distractions by keeping their hands quiet in order to concentrate on what is being said. These strategies designed for young learners are also good suggestions for all learners, because listening comprehension increases when the learner combines observation skills with focused attention on the message.

Listening takes place in two distinct situations: a. learners listen to audio input from recorded or live presentations with no opportunity for interaction; b. learners listen to someone in an exchange of information and ideas with the intention of responding and reacting immediately to what they hear. Lynch (1998) identifies these situations as "non-collaborative" or "collaborative." Collaborative situations involve two or more speakers and was discussed in the section on Interpersonal Communication. Non-collaborative refers to situations where there is no interaction between or among speakers. In this section we will focus on non-collaborative communication, characteristic of the Interpretive Mode, where the learners listen without the opportunity to negotiate meaning. This means that, in the case of "live" presentations such as speeches or plays, the learner has to capture as much meaning as possible from the messages "instantaneously." Understanding is influenced not only by the learner's proficiency in the target language, but also by the amount of background knowledge the learner has related to the topic.

It is important to distinguish comprehension from memory. Learners may not be able to indicate what they understood in a message simply because they don't remember what was said. In the case of movies, podcasts, or radio and television broadcasts, the learner may be able to stop, rewind and replay the recorded program to increase understanding. Research indicates that pausing a recording and repeating that recording are two of the most effective strategies to build listening comprehension (Rost, 2002). The strategies that follow are designed to help learners strengthen their abilities to listen, interpret, and analyze a variety of oral texts.

STRATEGY: Capturing and Keeping Messages

Learners are regularly involved as recipients of oral messages. Some examples of real-world situations where people have to capture and keep information include:

- Writing down opening and closing times in a recorded message for a store, a museum, a restaurant;
- Taking notes while attending a lecture or presentation;
- Writing down the pertinent details in a voicemail message;
- Listing key instructions someone gives to you, such as directions on how to get to a location in the city.

These types of activities help learners focus on the most important details in a spoken message or presentation, leaving out non-essential information.

STRATEGY: Focused Listening

The learner's ability to understand the main idea and supporting details in an oral text improves when the learner is familiar with the context. In introducing the listening activity, ask the learners to think about the vocabulary they might hear. Let learners listen multiple times to the same text so that they get used to the voice, the speed, and the accent of the speakers. Visual support is especially important for novice learners, and helpful for all learners. It is also important to direct the learners' attention to a single purpose for listening. For example, learners listen to a weather report in order to identify the mentioned cities or the temperatures. Give learners several images of different places in a city to identify as they hear them described or mentioned in order to say which city has the best weather for outdoor activities. When listening to a radio advertisement for a concert or festival, ask the learners to identify the location, the time, or the date for the event. As learners build their capacity to comprehend the spoken target language, ask them to listen for more information. For example, ask learners to sequence a series of pictures according to the order of events described in a news story. Have learners follow instructions on how to play a board game. Give them an outline to complete as they take a virtual tour of a museum such as the Hermitage in St. Petersburg, Russia.

All of these activities focus learners' attention on the important information contained in the text.

STRATEGY: Semi-scripted listening

Learners benefit from having a modified script of a listening text to follow as they listen, especially as they listen to longer texts. Think of the modified script as a way to keep the learner engaged in listening for information that expands or deepens their understanding of the text. If they get lost during listening, especially during a longer listening segment, they can get back on track when they locate where the speaker is in the script. A modified script can take the form of an outline to help the listener follow the main ideas. A modified script might give the first sentence of each paragraph in a lecture or presentation with space to take notes on the details that follow. There might be a series of images, such as the slides in a PowerPoint presentation to help focus the learner's attention. Again, learners can add notes to each slide. All of these strategies help learners stay tuned in rather than giving up and tuning out.

STRATEGY: Building listening skills through music

Listening to songs is another way to build listening skills. Listening to a song multiple times over the course of several days or weeks or months or years is not unusual. The tolerance for listening to a song multiple times makes it a powerful way to build listening skills. Websites like LyricsGap.com and LyricsTraining.com feature music from around the world with activities to build listening skills, including listening for the main idea of the song, or completing a cloze activity where the lyrics of the song are given to the learners with certain words missing. Learners listen to the song and fill in the missing words. Another app, Spotify, is a website for finding music from around the world. Instructors and learners can create and share playlists, locate the lyrics to songs, and follow people whose interests in music are similar to theirs. Asking learners to listen to a song as a homework assignment can be a refreshing and motivating way for learners to practice the target language outside of class. Their first assignment might be to listen for the main idea, and the mood conveyed through the sound of the song. In subsequent assignments, learners can listen for a phrase that repeats several times, for key vocabulary, or for a sequence of actions. After practicing how to listen to songs, small groups or pairs of learners can listen to different songs with a common theme. In class the learners compare their songs and how the artist(s) interpreted the theme.

Strategies Specific to Building Reading Skills

Reading in the target language provides language patterns, vocabulary, and content that learners can use to build Interpersonal and Presentational skills. Learners are more successful at reading when they feel that the text is personally relevant. Instructors who can connect what learners read in a World Language class to what they are studying in other classes, to their past experiences, and to their interests set the stage for successful reading experiences.

Establishing the purpose for reading allows readers to determine how to approach the text: do they need to read carefully for details, or do they only need to understand the big idea(s)? In either case, the purpose for reading a text should reflect real-world reading tasks as much as possible. For example, reading the front page of a newspaper may mean reading the headlines to gain a broad sense of what is happening in the world, and then selecting one article or more to read in detail based on personal interest. Reading a book with lots of photos of animals may mean that the reader spends more time looking at the photos, occasionally reading the text that accompanies the photos. With no expectation to be able to retell all the details about the animals, the purpose may simply be enjoyment. In both cases, reading purposes are real-world and personalized.

There is probably no better way to have learners practice the 3Ps (Cultures Goal) paradigm of Products (what is created by members of the culture), Practices (patterns of behavior accepted by a society), and Perspectives (traditional ideas, attitudes, meanings, and values) than to have them interpret the context and content of an authentic text. One of the most helpful developments for making this practice possible is the rise of the use of infographics in today's worldwide media. Infographics can be readily found on the Internet. A good resource for infographics is the Pinterest account for the Central States Conference on the Teaching of Foreign Languages (CSCTFL), at pinterest.com/CSCTFL. Infographics use visuals and brief descriptions that often link products to practices, opening the discussion to possible perspectives gained from the information. For example, look at the infographic in Figure 18 (see p. 42) that shows where people in France listen to music and what online sources they use most often to listen to music.

Figure 18. Music listening among French people

LA VOITURE, PREMIER LIEU D'ÉCOUTE

Écoutez-vous de la musique...

	Tous les jours ou presque	1 à 2 fois par semaine	moins souvent	Jamais
en voiture	65%	17%	9%	9%
à la maison	61%	24%	12%	3%
en dehors de chez vous	16%	19%	38%	26%
au travail	14%	8%	14%	64%
dans les transports	10%	7%	17%	66%
dans la rue	9%	8%	20%	64%

YOUTUBE, SITE PRÉFÉRÉ DES AUDITEURS

Écoutez-vous de la musique sur...

	Tous les jours ou presque	1 à 2 fois par semaine	moins souvent	Jamais
YouTube	22%	33%	31%	14%
Deezer	10%	18%	29%	42%
Site Internet d'une radio	8%	17%	23%	51%
Dailymotion	5%	12%	30%	53%
Spotify	3%	5%	9%	83%

Sondage Ipsos pour la Sacem, la Spré et Mood Media, réalisé du 30 octobre au 5 novembre 2013 auprès d'un échantillon représentatif de 2.003 personnes âgées de 16 ans et plus (méthode des quotas). Les interviews ont eu lieu par questionnaire autoadministré en ligne.

The product is music. The practice is where people listen to music and which online sources are used most often. Based on the graphic, the perspective to explore is how French people value music in their daily life. Questions an instructor might pose include:

- What do you want to know about the people who responded to the survey?
- What factors might influence the data represented on this infographic?
- How do you think your friends and family would respond to a question about where and how often they listen to music?

Even at the Novice level, learners can interpret the information displayed on this and other infographics. They can also suggest some cultural comparisons that lead to further exploration to determine if their suggestions are accurate.

STRATEGY: *Overview and Details*

- **Skim and Scan:** Learners may scan the text to locate specific information. Or they may skim the text to get its main idea. Both are valuable skills and, depending on the purpose for the text, learners may complete either or both strategies. In some cases, it is quite adequate to stop after skimming and/or scanning. In other cases, after gaining some initial impressions of the text, it may be appropriate to read the text for more details and tone, inferences, or cultural perspectives.
- **Eliminating non-essential information:** Rather than highlighting or underlining information the learners consider important to the understanding of a written text, ask them to cross out or highlight all lines that they believe are not important to their understanding of the text. Then ask them to use the lines that are not crossed out or highlighted to identify the main ideas of the text. The non-highlighted text can also be used for a Presentational task where the learner writes a summary of the text. If the learner was not successful in identifying the main ideas of the text using this strategy, it might signal that the text is too complex, or that the learner's background knowledge and/or vocabulary is too limited to successfully interpret the text.

STRATEGY: *Response Notebook*

A response notebook is another way to build learners' interpretive skills. By asking learners to write responses to questions that require analysis of the text, learners have time to reflect before composing a response. They also have the opportunity to try out a response they may not offer in front of the whole class. By exchanging their response with a classmate, they receive immediate feedback on what they wrote, along with some ideas on how to adjust their response. Figure 19 is a sample of a page in a response notebook.

Figure 19. Response notebook page

Name of text: ______________________

Question: ______________________

My response	*Partner response*

Before the learners read a text, the instructor poses an open-ended question designed to move learners beyond the literal to the interpretive level of the text. After reading the text, learners respond to the question in writing. Next, they exchange their notebooks with their partners. Their partners read the responses. Before writing a reaction, the instructor may model some ways learners may respond to what was written. The partners write their reactions in the notebook. They return the notebooks to the owners, who read the comments. At this point the instructor may lead a full-class discussion about the question. After the discussion, learners may adjust their responses by adding to or expanding on their original response. Some suggestions for questions are:

- Was the title of the story/book/poem/article a good one? Why or why not?
- How would you describe the author's style of writing? What do you like/dislike about the style? Give examples.
- How did the end of the story make you feel? Give examples from the story to support your response. Would you change the end of the story if you could? Why or why not?

Another option to reacting to an entire text is to focus on a single quote related to the theme and topic the learners are studying. Here is a quote from Picasso to accompany a unit on art: *"Todo niño es un artista. Lo difícil está en seguir siéndolo cuando creces."* (Every child is an artist. The problem is how to remain an artist once we grow up.) Learners respond to the quote by explaining what, in their opinion, Picasso meant. They need to justify their response with examples from their personal experiences, from their observations of others, and from what they learned during the unit. Again, the learners write their responses in their journals, exchange them for reaction, and then write their final responses.

STRATEGY: Reading logs

There are several ways on the Web for learners to track what they read digitally instead of using a paper reading log. We recommend a tool like Stackup.net. Instructors load the links to websites they want their learners to read during free reading time, as a homework assignment, or for personal interest (example: http://www.elmundo.es/). Learners sign up on the Stackup website using their Google accounts. They will be prompted to build a profile page that will keep track of the articles they read and how long they spend reading. They can also indicate their favorite topics. Complete information and easy-to-follow instructions are on the Stackup website.

Strategies Specific to Building Viewing Skills

"It is as important to be visually literate, to understand pictures and how they affect us, as it is to be word-literate." (Bill Kennedy, Toledo Museum of Art) A first reaction to the concept of viewing might bring to mind video clips and movies, and they certainly do qualify as Interpretive communication. But viewing also includes images, photos, art, architecture, and advertisements. All of these examples communicate messages, and the interpretation draws strongly from cultural understanding. Visual literacy is defined as the ability to understand, interpret and evaluate visual messages (Bristor & Drake, 1994). Genelle Morain (1976) defines visual literacy from the world languages perspective: "...being able to read the visual aspects of one's surroundings. Someone who is visually literate is able to recognize the natural and manmade symbols around one and interpret their meanings in the same way as those who live in that environment would interpret them."

It can be argued that a visual without words does not fit in the Interpretive mode. However, it can also be argued that instructors encourage learners to use drawings and gestures to communicate messages. And we tell learners to sharpen their observation skills to strengthen their comprehension. Thinking back to the cave paintings at Lascaux, France, generations of people have visited those caves to read the images and try to unlock their meanings. Images have always been used as a means of communication, and in today's visually rich environment, learning how to interpret images in their cultural context is a valuable tool for language learners.

STRATEGY: Maximizing the potential of video

Films and videos of all sorts provide visual support to the commentary, facilitating understanding of the messages communicated. Films and video bring the cultural context for the messages to life. Learners actually see the places where the target language is spoken instead of depending on their imagination. They see native speakers interacting in those places to gain insights into the cultural behaviors that accompany the spoken messages. Recommendations about the optimum length for showing a video clip vary. Some researchers suggest that careful selection of clips as short as 30 seconds to a maximum of four minutes allows learners to focus intently on the verbal and visual messages. Others recommend that a clip of 10-15 minutes can be very effective for telling a story. Showing a film for an entire class period or over several class periods is generally not recommended. Longer films can be shown after class or as part of a language club activity. For certain films, instructors may invite learners, their parents, and friends for a night at the movies and show the film with subtitles, followed by a discussion of the film's significance within the target culture and the universality of the film's theme.

When the visual context of a video is rich, it is helpful to show the clip without sound the first time. This way learners can focus attention on the visual clues in the clip. After viewing the clip, learners can make predictions about the main idea of the clip and what the people in the video might be saying. They can discuss what they noticed about the different scenes in the clip. The second time, they can watch the video with sound to verify their predictions. Films with subtitles can help learners understand the commentary. Subtitles clarify speech that is difficult to understand. Based on the language level of the learners, instructors determine if showing subtitles is helpful, and if the subtitles are most helpful in English or in the target language.

STRATEGY: Reading photos, images, art, architecture

Visual support is critical to understanding the target language, especially for novice learners. Asking the question "What do you see?" helps learners become more observant of the clues to meaning that are found in photos and images. For example, as learners enter class, they might see a photo of a family in Cairo eating a meal. Their first task is to work with a partner to describe as much as they can in response to "What do you see?" For beginners, their responses might begin with colors, objects, people. What they can express in the target language may be much more limited than what they notice in the photo. In this case, they could complete a journal entry, listing as many things as they can in the target language, and then continuing in English with what else they noticed in the photo. Asking learners to complete a sentence that begins with "I wonder..." encourages curiosity and underlines the importance and power of observation to deepen their understanding of the target language and culture.

Instructors can use the journal entries as springboards to class discussions and further exploration of a topic. The entries provide insights into how learners have interpreted an image. The instructor can clarify misconceptions and expand on topics of interest to the learners. Creative Commons includes a search page for locating Creative Commons-licensed images, music, video, and multimedia at www.search.creativecommons.org. These images include guidelines for use with appropriate acknowledgement as stipulated by the owner of the image. The University of Texas at Austin (http://laits.utexas.edu/lescant/) and MIT (www.realiaproject.org) have collections of open source images for use in world language classrooms.

STRATEGY: Using images as a springboard to communication

Table 10 is based on strategies from Project Zero Harvard Graduate School of Education and adapted for world language instruction. Each strategy begins with an image and is accompanied by a brief outline of the questions or process to implement, and the purpose for the strategy.

The importance of the Interpretive Mode. The preceding selection of strategies is designed to increase learners' ability to interpret oral, written, and visual texts. It is a sampling intended to remind instructors to move beyond the literal level of comprehension to engage learners in critical thinking as they explore cultural products, practices, and perspectives reflected through the texts, and the author's intent for creating the text. The more opportunities learners have to read, listen, and view authentic texts, the more their own writing and speaking in the target language will improve because of the influence of multiple models of language native speakers use to express themselves. ***Additional activities to build Interpretive communication skills are in Appendix E.***

IDEA-SHARING

The Interpretive Standard asks learners to understand, interpret, and analyze what is heard, read, or viewed. In order to interpret and analyze a message, learners need to consider the cultural context for the message. Share ways that you can draw learners' attention to the cultural context and its influence on the message (reading between the lines).

Table 10. Using images as springboards to communication

Strategy	Technique	Purpose
Questioning and investigating	See / Think / Wonder • What do you see? • What do you think about what you see? • What do you wonder?	Allows learners to distinguish between observations and interpretations. Stimulates curiosity, and encourages logical guessing.
Observing and describing	Beginning / Middle / End • If this artwork/image is the beginning of a story, what might happen next? • If this artwork/image is the middle of a story, what might have happened before? What might happen next? • If this artwork/image is the end of the story, what might the story be about?	Allows learners to use narrative to elaborate and extend ideas based on images.
Comparing and contrasting	Headlines • Invent headlines for two works of art or two photos that capture contrasts in the images.	Allows learners to identify and clarify big ideas.
Finding Complexity	Parts/Purposes/Complexities • What is the main message of this photo? • What are the supporting details? • Why was the photo taken?	Allows learners to consider the composition of a photo and various ways in which a photo is complex.
Exploring viewpoints	Step Inside—Perceive / Know / Care About • Take on the character of the thing or person you've chosen in the photo or painting • Speak as though you are the thing or person • Talk about who you are, what you are, what you are experiencing.	Allows learners to consider things from a different viewpoint, bringing abstract concepts, pictures and events to life.
Reasoning	What makes you say that? • What's going on in this sequence of images? • What do you see that makes you say that?	Allows learners to describe what they see and know, build explanations, promoting evidence-based reasoning.

The Presentational Mode: Presenting Ideas to Diverse Audiences Using Appropriate Media

Presentational Mode of Communication "Learners present information, concepts, and ideas to inform, explain, persuade, and narrate on a variety of topics using appropriate media and adapting to various audiences of listeners, readers, or viewers."

In the Presentational Mode, learners create products via writing or speaking for an audience. Because the learners will share information with others, more sophisticated and accurate language is expected, and the content has to be well-organized. Examples of products that learners create include writing original stories, creating websites, giving prepared speeches, designing infographics, or making podcasts. It is important to note that, in order to meet this World-Readiness Standard, learners must consider the intended audience and the appropriate media they will use to deliver their message. Consideration of audience and appropriate media is also part of 21st-century literacies. The characteristics of the Presentational Mode are listed in Table 11 (see p. 46).

The Presentational Mode encourages learners to be reflective communicators. The characteristics of this mode highlight the importance of thoughtful preparation of messages, either in writing or orally. The Presentational Mode allows learners to showcase their best speaking and writing skills, skills made stronger because the learners have time to reflect on their messages, and to edit them based on their own proofreading and on the constructive feedback of others.

A major role of the Presentational Mode is to give learners time to work with the language and content they are learning in order to create a real-world product that can be shared with an audience outside the classroom. It is through this emphasis on creating a polished product for an audience that learners gain the

Table 11. Characteristics of Presentational Communication

Presentational Communication	
Is Not	**Is**
Two-way communication	One-way communication
Speaking or writing only for the instructor	Speaking or writing for audiences within and beyond the classroom
Culture-neutral	Awareness of the cultural background and knowledge of the audience
Prepared in isolation	Improved through feedback from peers, instructors, other interested reviewers
Unedited, unpracticed	Practiced, rehearsed, polished, edited
Random thoughts	Planned, organized
A single draft with no proofreading	Improved by using appropriate tools: dictionary, spell check, peer review

dispositions of perseverance, attention to detail, and desire for excellence valued by employers in all sectors of the work world.

Fred Newmann (1996) from the University of Wisconsin advocates for authenticity in learning. He explains authenticity by stating that learners must apply the facts, concepts, and skills they learn into the construction of some knowledge product or new understanding. They must develop an in-depth understanding and clearly communicate the content. The performance must have value personally or be of value beyond the educational institution. It is not simply to be used to rate learners for grading purposes. The performance must be shared in a meaningful way with audiences outside the classroom.

When thinking about the Presentational Mode, instructors need to have a clear understanding of the balance between the ***process*** of creating the presentation and the actual ***product*** or presentation that results from the process. Consider the ***process*** as the learning phase where learners create rough drafts of the product they want to showcase. They receive feedback from their peers, their instructor, and other interested people. Based on the feedback, learners make adjustments to the draft of their project to improve the quality. This may include making a series of revisions before arriving at the final ***product,*** beginning with the value of the content, and followed by the accuracy of the language used. When the final ***product*** is polished, reflecting the best performance of the learner, it is ready to be shared with an audience outside the classroom. When the ***product*** is shared, the evaluation shifts to a holistic appreciation of the quality of the product. The learner has benefited from creating an original presentation and receiving feedback to improve it, both in terms of overall content and message and in terms of language control. Having worked for an extended time period on a presentation helps cement the content and language in the mind of the learner.

While preparing a polished performance is fundamental to the Presentational Mode, there are times when the instructor may choose to have learners prepare "on demand" performances rather than spending extended time to create a polished performance. "On demand" performances give the instructor and learners evidence of what the learners can do independently without any outside help.

The ACTFL Performance Descriptors (2015) outline the characteristics of texts that learners can produce in the Presentational Mode at the Novice, Intermediate, and Advanced levels. Table 12 describes the Parameters of Performance: Functions, Content/Context, and Text Type.

Presentational Writing Strategies

STRATEGY: Replicating a model text

The earliest stages of writing focus on copying words correctly in meaningful contexts. Examples include writing the day and date at the top of an assignment, keeping a vocabulary notebook drawing and labeling pictures that represent the new

Table 12. Presentational Performance Descriptors: Parameters of Performance

Presentational Mode			
Domain	**Novice**	**Intermediate**	**Advanced**
Overview	Communicates information on very familiar topics using a variety of words, phrases, and sentences that have been practiced and memorized.	Communicates information and expresses own thoughts about familiar topics using sentences and series of sentences.	Communicates information and expresses self with detail and organization on familiar and some new concrete topics using paragraphs.
Functions	Presents simple, basic, information on very familiar topics by producing words, lists, notes, and formulaic language using highly practiced language. May show emerging evidence of the ability to express own thoughts and preferences.	Expresses own thoughts and presents information and personal preferences on familiar topics by creating with language primarily in present time. May show emerging evidence of the ability to tell or retell a story and provide additional description.	Produces narrations and descriptions in all major time frames on familiar and some unfamiliar topics. May show emerging evidence of the ability to provide a well-supported argument, including detailed evidence in support of a point of view.
Contexts/Content	Creates messages in some personally relevant contexts on topics that relate to basic biographical information. May show emerging evidence of the ability to create messages in highly practiced contexts related to oneself and immediate surroundings.	Creates messages in contexts relevant to oneself, others, and one's immediate environment. May show emerging evidence of the ability to create messages on general interest and work-related topics.	Creates messages fully and effectively in contexts both personal and general. Content areas include topics of personal and general interest (community, national, and international events) as well as work-related topics and areas of special competence. May show emerging evidence of the ability to create messages in more abstract content areas.
Text Type	Produces words and phrases and highly practiced sentences or formulaic questions.	Produces sentences, series of sentences, and some connected sentences.	Produces full paragraphs that are organized and detailed.

ACTFL Performance Descriptors (2015)

words, and writing sentences that use the new words. As learners' ability to express themselves grows, they write for more purposes and audiences. Past experiences reading and writing will influence how well learners write in the target language. Here is a process that helps learners successfully complete a writing assignment. For this writing assignment, learners need to write a biographical sketch.

1. Begin by sharing an example of a biographical sketch with the learners. Take time to point out organizational features, types of information included, specialized vocabulary, and sentence patterns.
2. Hand out other examples of biographical sketches, and have the learners work in pairs or small groups to look for and highlight organizational features, information that is included, specialized vocabulary, and sentence patterns. Post the highlighted biographical sketches on the walls of the classroom. Learners move around the room, looking at the sketches and the highlighted features. After the learners return to their seats, the instructor discusses commonalities and unique features among the sketches.
3. Now the class works together to write a biographical sketch of someone they have studied. The instructor acts as scribe, writing down ideas from the class. After the ideas are collected, the instructor guides a discussion of how to put the ideas together to create a biographical sketch. The class and instructor write the sketch together.
4. The learners are now ready to individually write drafts of biographical sketches of well-known people from the target cultures.

STRATEGY: Researching content

The ability to efficiently access and evaluate information from multiple sources is an expectation of 21st-century literacies. Learners need to learn how to explore the vast resources on the Internet efficiently in order to find credible information that reflects a variety of viewpoints. Instructors can facilitate learners' research by providing them with a few websites as starting points for their exploration of a topic. As learners move beyond these recommended sites, they can become critical consumers by asking these three questions about the websites they find:

1. How trustworthy is the reputation of the author of the website?
2. How trustworthy is the reputation of the publisher of the website?

3. Who is the audience for the website?
4. How recently has the website been updated?
5. Do other websites independently confirm the information found on one website?

Whenever learners are researching a problem that involves another country, they can make use of country codes and/or advanced Google searches to limit their search to a particular country. A list of country codes can be found at CountryCode.org. Finally, proper documentation of websites used in preparing presentations is essential, and another requirement for literacy in the 21st century. Many websites provide up-to-date guides on how to cite resources, with special attention to electronic resources.

STRATEGY: Peer review

Modeling and practice are necessary prerequisites for learners to become helpful peer reviewers for their classmates. After learners complete a rough draft of a writing assignment, it is time for them to receive a first round of constructive feedback. The first round focuses on message, not mechanics. Before learners give feedback to classmates, the instructor models appropriate feedback for the class by projecting the first page of a sample draft on the classroom screen. After reading the sample, the instructor leads learners through a think-aloud about the draft, asking and responding to questions about the message. With each question, the instructor invites learners to respond to the question, and to justify their responses by giving examples from the sample draft:

1. What is the main idea of this writing?
2. What supporting details did the author provide?
3. After reading this text, what questions do you have about the message?
4. What suggestions do you have for the author to make the text stronger? Consider:
    a. Organization
    b. Details
    c. Descriptions

After modeling how to comment on the model text, have the learners work in pairs, reviewing their drafts, and making comments following the sequence the instructor modeled. The authors can now edit their drafts as appropriate to the content of their presentation before focusing on the accuracy of the target language.

Peers are most effective in reviewing each other's drafts in terms of the target language use when they have specific tasks to review. For example, given a checklist of non-negotiables (required elements) that are part of the instructions for completion of the presentation, a peer could verify that the non-negotiables were met. Non-negotiables can be very specific, because the learner has time to determine how to incorporate them into the presentation. They may include both linguistic and formatting elements to guide learners to create a finished product ready to be evaluated. Simply including the non-negotiables is not part of the evaluation or grading of learners' performance. Figure 20 is an example of a list of non-negotiables for a 3-paragraph essay about "A remarkable artist."

Figure 20. Checklist of non-negotiables

"A Remarkable Artist" Non-negotiables

- **Title**
- **3 paragraphs**
- **Word-processed**
- **2 examples of comparisons**
- **2 examples of making recommendations or opinions**
- **3 examples of Priority Vocabulary**

Learners can also be helpful in giving feedback to peers about specific grammatical structures, especially those that were highly practiced during a unit of instruction. For example, they could verify adjective placement and agreement if the language function emphasized during the unit was *describing people, places, or things*. When learning how to proofread, a first step is to locate all the examples of the grammatical point they are checking and underline or highlight the examples. Place a star over any example that needs correction. Instructors can quickly check to see if the proofreader has identified all the examples of the grammar point, and if the starred examples do need attention. This serves as a formative assessment for the proofreader, and establishes accountability for the proofreader. Taking time to develop peer editing skills among learners is worthwhile in giving learners valuable and immediate feedback from more than just the instructor. More important is that it develops the learners' proofreading skills for their own work. Instructors need to discuss and practice with learners how to give meaningful feedback while being sensitive to the feelings of the person receiving the feedback. One paradigm is to give both "warm" (I like how you...) and "cool" (Have you thought about/considered...?) comments as feedback.

STRATEGY: Building Vocabulary

There is an adage that says you can tell that someone is well-read by the way that he or she speaks or writes. This refers not only to the breadth and depth of topics a person can discuss but also to the variety of sentence structures used, and specificity of vocabulary that is integrated. For most language learners, memorizing a list of words and their translations is not an effective way to build vocabulary.

- **Multiple exposures to new words.** For new words to become part of learners' active vocabulary, the learners need to see and use the words in multiple contexts over time. Drawing a visual and/or making up a gesture to represent the new word, and connecting the new word and image to a personally meaningful sentence, helps learners remember the new words. Keep a word bank of five to seven new words on a wall in the classroom, with reminders to the learners to try to incorporate one or several of these new words every time they write or say something. Learners can incorporate these words in their journal writing. They can look for examples of the word used in context and post those on the class website or on a graffiti wall in the classroom. Using the new word frequently in meaningful contexts helps make the word easy to retrieve as it becomes part of the learners' long-term memory. Select and practice vocabulary based on the way the learners need to use the new words:
  - Do the learners need to use the word actively, or recognize its context?
  - How frequently will learners see this word?
  - How frequently will learners use this word?

With these questions in mind, instructors can make informed decisions about the words that build learners' ability to communicate effectively in the target language.

STRATEGY: Building Sentences and Paragraphs

- **Word Splash:** Select seven to ten vocabulary words or phrases related to the theme or topic, and splash them on the interactive whiteboard or screen. Learners choose from among the words in the splash to write sentences related to the topic of the unit. With careful selection of the words for the splash, the task could be to create a paragraph, respond to a question, imagine a story or create a sequence of events or a step-by-step process. Figure 21 shows a word splash about the choice of classes and success in school based on the essential question, "How does school prepare us for the future?"

Figure 21. Word splash about school.

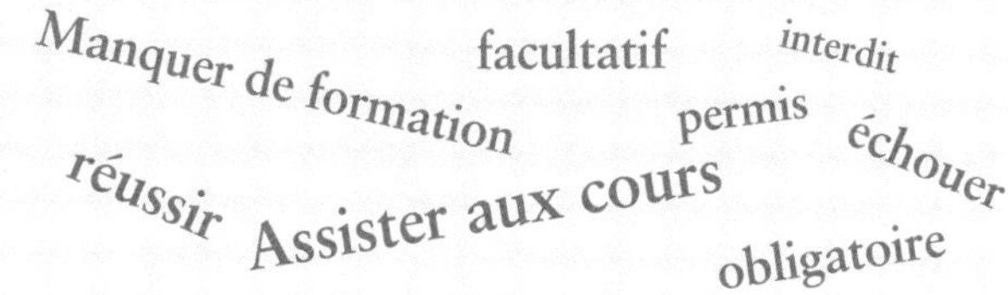

(Word splash vocabulary: to lack preparation, elective, forbidden, allowed, to pass or succeed, to attend classes, to fail, required)

- **Think – write – pair – share – write:** Learners benefit from multiple opportunities to practice writing and to receive feedback on their writing. In this model, the instructor gives a prompt to the class and asks them to think about how they can respond to the prompt. Next, they write their thoughts, then exchange them with a partner. After that, two pairs of learners exchange their writings, sharing ideas and suggestions with each other. Finally, the learners take their thoughts and what they learned from others' comments during sharing, and write a final response to the prompt. This final response could be an "on demand" sample of their writing, or it could be a draft that is a starting point for an essay to be polished.
- **Sentence starters:** Especially for novice learners, it is helpful to give sentence starters for learners to complete. If, for example, the learners are writing about a famous artist, these sentence starters might be helpful:
  - She is famous because....
  - Her murals tell the stories of....
  - You can see her murals at....
- **Sequencing:** Learners are given five to seven sentences to put in a logical order. The sentences could be related to steps in making something. They could be instructions in how to play a game. They might retell an event or incident or story. Next, learners add connecting words to strengthen the flow of information. It is sometimes helpful if images accompany the sentences to give learners more ideas on how to add details to make the sequence more cohesive.

Presentational Speaking Strategies

STRATEGY: Reduce anxiety in speaking for an audience

Speaking for an audience is often accompanied by varying degrees of anxiety, which is multiplied when communicating in the target language. With a much smaller storehouse of active vocabulary, it is hard to "punt" when a word is forgotten or an idea is lost. Learners benefit from giving presentations in small groups before presenting to a large group. Even these small group presentations can be daunting for learners. Once again, technology can provide scaffolding to prepare learners to present to an audience.

- **Individual practice:** Using programs like Audacity and Google Voice, learners can practice pronunciation by recording their voices as they imitate a native speaker, then comparing their pronunciation to the native speaker's pronunciation. Audacity also provides an excellent opportunity to offer language students a comparative analysis of their own spoken work with that of their native-speaking instructor. The Audacity interface includes a basic spectrograph of audio files. By loading a student's spoken audio file and a native speaker's audio file, students can listen and view the differences between the audio samples. With a visual and auditory representation of spoken language, learners can better recognize the differences. Practice becomes purposeful as learners match their pronunciation to a model.
- **Small group practice:** It is helpful to build confidence in learners by having the audience focus on something other than the person speaking. One way to do this is to give a small group of learners a ball of yarn. The yarn has ribbons tied into it at different intervals. A topic is given to the group to discuss. The first person begins winding the yarn into a new ball, talking about the assigned topic until he or she arrives at a ribbon. The yarn is passed to the next person who continues to talk about the topic until he or she arrives at another ribbon. In this example of scaffolding, learners speak individually in front of a small audience that is focusing on the ball of yarn and not on the person speaking. In fact, the person speaking is also focusing on the ball of yarn. This activity is a first step in building confidence to speak in front of an audience.
- **Readers Theatre:** Learners take different roles in a play or story that they read aloud together, providing an engaging and motivating context for practicing reading aloud. It is a way for learners to build their confidence in speaking alone in front of an audience, while also practicing their pronunciation and fluency. They use their voices, facial expressions, and gestures to become the characters in the reading selection. At times, they may even have a symbolic prop such as a hat, a cane, glasses, a long scarf to remind the audience of the character's identity. There is considerable research in support of readers theatre as a way to develop fluency and interest in reading from literacy development experts (Slavin, 1987; Griffith & Rasinski, 2004; Young & Rasinski, 2009). Carrick (2006) states that, through repeated readings, learners increase their ability to decode words quickly and accurately, and to read with greater ease. Comprehension also increases with repeated readings (Pikulsi & Chard, 2005). Curtain & Dahlberg (2016) note that reading aloud is useful when there is a real-world purpose to the reading. Readers Theatre brings a text to life as learners assume the roles of the characters and the narrator, performing for an audience.

The importance of the Presentational Mode: The Presentational Mode provides the space for learners to work on increasing their accuracy and style using the target language. They benefit from feedback concerning both content and grammar as they work toward a polished final product they will share with an audience beyond the classroom. It is an opportunity for learners to showcase their best writing and speaking with pride in their accomplishments. ***Additional activities to build Presentational communication skills are in Appendix F.***

> IDEA-SHARING
>
> The Presentational Mode requires that learners use appropriate media to present various topics to an audience. When learners know that people beyond their classmates are going to read or hear their presentations, motivation increases to create high-quality products. Share ideas on potential audiences and the kinds of presentations that would be of interest to them.

Summary: To be successful communicators in a world language, learners must be surrounded by opportunities to hear and practice the target language, and receive timely and meaningful feedback on their work. They need to be able to exchange ideas in conversations (Interpersonal Mode). They need to understand and interpret a wide variety of oral, written, and visual texts (Interpretive Mode). They need to be able to present ideas and concepts for an audience using appropriate media (Presentational Mode). When planning a unit of instruction, identify how the three modes of communication can be integrated and practiced throughout the unit.

Reflect on the essential question: What kinds of instructional strategies build effective communication?

Analyze an example about a difference in teaching methods between two instructors.

A colleague understands the characteristics of the three modes of communication but believes that learners cannot engage in tasks related to three modes until they have learned the grammatical structures of the target language. To that end, learners spend class time completing worksheets on discrete grammatical points and translating sentences from English into the target language. How can you show that grammar is only a tool that helps learners complete purposeful communicative tasks? For example, your colleague just completed a thematic unit on music. Rather than leading with a discussion of personal preferences in music, the instructor started the unit by telling the class that they were going to learn how to make regular and irregular comparisons of adjectives in order to talk about music. Learners received a list of adjectives in the target language and had to write the meanings of as many as they knew. Then the instructor modeled how to make a regular comparison: *The song is long. This song is longer.* The learners received a worksheet with twenty statements. For each statement, the learners wrote a comparison statement. The rest of the unit continued in much the same way, with learners practicing regular and irregular comparisons, and then how to write superlative statements. Near the end of the unit, the instructor played some music from the target culture and asked the learners to work in pairs to compare the music to the music they like. What suggestions would you give your colleague on how to use the grammatical focus as a tool to focus on purposeful communication?

Apply ideas to your practice using the knowledge gained from the chapter.

Think of a lesson you teach, and determine if all three modes of communication are reflected in the lesson. If all three modes are not included, is there a way to add in missing modes?

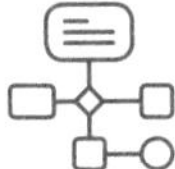

Extend your learning by completing these activities.

1. Think of one of the units you teach, and design a task for each mode of communication based on the suggestions in this chapter.
2. Using the following template and an authentic text you have identified for one of the units you teach, identify pre-, during, and post-activities to support the use of the text.

Text title: ______			
Circle:	Listening	Reading	Viewing

   a. Generate possible activities to complete before exploring the text. These activities prepare learners for what they are going to listen to, read, or view.
   b. Generate possible activities to complete as learners explore the text. These activities relate directly to the text, and learners complete them as they explore the text.
   c. Generate possible activities to complete after learners explore the text. These activities help learners verify their understanding of the text, analyze the text, and make inferences based on the text.
3. Consider three similarities between the Interpretive skills of listening and reading and three differences:

Similarities	Differences
Understanding increases when background knowledge is elicited.	Listening occurs quickly, often without repetition. Reading allows for rereading.

4. Obtain a copy of *Implementing Integrated Performance Assessment* (ACTFL, 2013) for further information about the three modes of communication. Challenge yourself to create an integrated performance assessment (IPA) for a unit you teach.

Deepen your knowledge by exploring additional resources.

Adair-Hauck, B., Glisan, E., & Troyan, F. (2013). *Implementing Integrated Performance Assessment.* Alexandria, VA: ACTFL.

Curtain, H., & Dahlberg, C. (2016). *Languages and Learners Making the Match: World Language Instruction in K–8 Classrooms and Beyond.* Boston, MA: Pearson.

Paesani, K., Allen, H.W., & Dupuy, B. (2015). *A Multiliteracies Framework for Collegiate Foreign Language Teaching.* Upper Saddle River, NJ: Pearson.

Shrum, J., & Glisan, E. (2015). *Teacher's handbook, contextualized language instruction.* Cengage Learning.

Chapter 4 Engaging All Learners: Independence and Collaboration

How Do the Strategies I Choose Encourage Both Independence and Collaboration?

- Strategies to Develop Independent and Autonomous Learners
- Strategies to Facilitate Cooperation and Collaboration Among Learners

"Above all, I believe that language study offers our students an experience they can't get elsewhere. In a world language classroom, learners are fully engaged in meaningful, personalized activities that promote proficiency in the target language and its culture. They have the opportunity to delve into individual interests such as art, music, cooking, design, architecture, linguistics, history, and current political, social and environmental issues. Businesses heavily recruit employees with these broader cultural sensitivities, as they are more flexible in a changing work force, and I would submit, are more interesting people."

—Lisa Lilley, ACTFL Teacher of the Year 2010

The overarching goal for world language instruction is to actively engage all learners in "developing competence to communicate effectively and interact with cultural competence to participate in multilingual communities at home and around the world" (The National Standards Collaborative Board, 2015, p. 11). Let's look at what it means "to actively engage all learners" as a starting point for this chapter. The Great Schools Partnership Glossary of Education Reform (2016) defines student engagement as: "the degree of attention, curiosity, interest, optimism, and passion that students show when they are learning or being taught, which extends to the level of motivation they have to learn and progress in their education."

Learner engagement is an ongoing topic for research and discussion at all levels of instruction. The National Survey on Student Engagement designed for college students, the High School Survey of Student Engagement, and the newly released Middle Grades Survey of Student Engagement developed by The Center for Evaluation and Education Policy at Indiana University, Bloomington, provide insights into the strategies that engage learners. Another resource, *The Highly Engaged Classroom* (Marzano, Pickering & Heflebower, 2010), summarizes key research about learner engagement and recommendations for classroom practice. These resources present a wide variety of classroom instructional strategies designed to engage all learners. For this publication, we have highlighted several strategies that can be broadly categorized as ones that encourage independence and ones that encourage collaboration. A first reaction is that these two qualities are diametrically opposed to each other. However, upon reflection, the two categories actually complement each other. Together they acknowledge the importance of learners making individual choices about what they learn and how they learn, monitoring their own on-task behaviors and progress toward task completion, and then self-assessing the quality of their work. Successful collaboration depends on the active engagement of participants who are prepared to share their knowledge and skills with others, monitor their on-task behaviors and progress toward task completion as a responsible group member, and identify ways to improve the quality of the final group product. The qualities needed to be a successful independent learner are also needed for successful collaboration.

Jackson & Zmuda (2014), in their article on learner engagement, identify personal relevance, classroom culture, challenging work, and clarity as keys to successful engagement. Classroom culture, personal relevance, and challenging work are discussed in other parts of this publication. Let's turn our attention to what is meant by clarity. Jackson & Zmuda describe clarity as making sure that all learners understand what they need to do to successfully complete an assignment or participate in an activity, and how completing the assignment or activity will help them successfully meet the unit goals and objectives. Evaluators in K–16 classrooms note that learners often politely go through the motions of completing an assignment or participating in an activity without really understanding what they are doing or why. One way to address this issue is to keep the essential question for the unit of instruction, along with the unit goals, front and center to help both the learners and instructor stay focused on the overarching goals for the unit. All unit activities and assignments should focus on purposeful use of the target language to respond to the essential question and achieve the unit goals. For example, a unit for Novice High Mandarin language learners is based on the essential question: *How green is my lifestyle?* During the unit, learners explore the impact of what they do daily on the environment. They describe what they do each day, and compare what they do to what their peers do in China. They complete calculations to measure their carbon footprints based on their daily routines. They compare their carbon footprints to footprints from around the world. They read articles suggesting how to reduce carbon footprints. They create a list of ways they can reduce their carbon footprints and what their school, family, and community can do. By continuously asking the question, "Why are the learners doing this activity?" instructors select only the activities that help learners respond to the essential question and demonstrate achievement of the unit goals. They will choose new vocabulary, language functions, and related structures that expand learners' ability to communicate about what is needed for a green lifestyle. Learning is focused and productive, relevant, and cognitively engaging. Learners are motivated to participate in class activities and to complete assignments because the purpose is clear, the instructions are clear, and how to be successful is clear. Clarity is fundamental to engaging all learners.

Carol Ann Tomlinson (2000) states that adjusting instruction to reflect the individual needs of learners should be done to facilitate "maximum student growth and individual success." To actively engage all learners so they are able to achieve the most important goals of a unit of instruction, Tomlinson suggests that instructors differentiate *content*, *process*, and/or *product*. *Content* differentiation is characterized by the level of detail in facts, language structures, and vocabulary that learners need to know to successfully meet the goals of instruction. *Process* differentiation considers the type of activities that will help learners achieve understanding of the content. *Product* differentiation gives learners options in how to demonstrate what they know and are able to do based on the learning in the unit of instruction. The two examples that follow are examples of differentiation in action, one at the post-secondary level and one at the elementary level.

A university professor of Arabic asked learners to work in small groups to explore different time periods in the history of Jordan. Learners gathered information about their assigned time period by using the Internet to access documents, photos, artwork, and videos. They processed the information they had collected by sharing written notes on the content via Google Docs, discussing the main ideas they found in their small group, and creating a graphic organizer for the key ideas and concepts. Learners made individual choices concerning the authentic texts they chose to read, listen to, or view. As a small group, they decided what information to share and how to share it with the rest of the class. In a final classroom discussion, the entire class synthesized the information from each time period into a final impression about the enduring importance of the various time periods. Differentiation allowed all learners to participate in the same project, consulting different types of resources on topics of personal interest within the time period. Individuals were able to determine how to share their findings with the class. The project design began with individuals in small groups choosing the aspect of the assigned time period they wanted to explore. Individually, the learners investigated their topic. They came back together as a group to decide how to organize and present their findings. The final presentation to the class involved all group members. The project successfully integrated independent learning with collaboration.

In an elementary Japanese immersion classroom, a unit based on the theme of Global Challenges, examined the question: How do natural disasters in one country impact the entire world? This unit was based on a science unit in Grade 5 about weather and natural disasters. Learners explored the effects of natural disasters in Japan. Some learners watched videos on the Internet, some read stories and poems children wrote about their experiences, and some reviewed photo journals created by reporters and schools in Japan. The class worked together to create a timeline about natural disasters in Japan over the past 50 years. Using what they learned about the number and types of natural disasters, some learners chose to record a PowerPoint presentation to upload to their school website. Some chose to create a display for a showcase in their school. Some made a video news report with a focus on how Japan prepares for natural disasters. Some wrote a story based on living in a place after a natural disaster. The choice of how to share what they learned opened the door to the creativity of the learners, allowing them to showcase knowledge and skills in a way that drew on their talents and interests.

In both of these examples, differentiation of content, process, and product provided paths for all learners to be successful in meeting the unit goals. In both situations, learners had opportunities to work alone and in groups.

Tomlinson emphasizes that differentiation is not a strategy but a mindset that guides instructors as they plan daily lessons and units that offer choices for all learners. Keep in mind Tomlinson's three categories of differentiation: content, process, product. Learners can access content through a variety of written materials in different formats, by watching videos, by examining photos, artwork, graphs, and charts, or by listening to someone tell a story or explain a concept, or demonstrate how to do something. In terms of process, instructors can plan a variety of individual and group activities that draw on different intelligences to practice listening, speaking, reading, and writing. Finally, in terms of product, learners can choose how they share what they have learned with others. Allowing learners to suggest how they want to demonstrate their learning honors the learner's interests and talents, and increases motivation to create a product of high quality.

The strategies included in this chapter are divided into two categories: engaging the learner as an individual to develop independent and autonomous learners, and engaging the learner as a member of a group to facilitate cooperation and collaboration. These two aspects of engagement could be considered the foundation of differentiation, providing opportunities for learners to work alone at their own pace and accommodating individual learning styles, while also including activities that depend on collaboration. Learners need to develop the ability to function independently at times and collaboratively at other times for success in school and beyond.

Strategies to Develop Independent and Autonomous Learners

Throughout this publication, we have stated that today's learners are motivated to learn when they find personal relevance in what they are learning. Exploring topics of personal interest on personal timelines are high priorities for them. While those characteristics are focused on the individual, they do not imply that the person is an independent or autonomous learner.

Independent learning is not to be interpreted as learners working alone. Independent learners have the ability to take charge of their own learning (Meyer, Haywood, Sachdev, & Faraday, 2008). Independence develops over time as a process of gradual transfer of responsibility for learning from the instructor to the learner. Instructors provide opportunities for learners to set goals and self-assess their progress toward meeting those goals. They offer options for how learners practice the target language, monitoring and providing immediate feedback on learners' on-task behaviors. In distinguishing independent learners from autonomous learners, some researchers state that independent learners work within a classroom structure, following the established curriculum, but they are able to work alone and in small groups without continuous monitoring by the instructor. They can determine what has to be done to complete a task without waiting for the instructor to give the next steps.

Autonomous learners are expected to assume greater responsibility for their own learning than independent learners. Dam (1990) and Holec (1983) state that people qualify as autonomous learners when they:

- independently choose aims and purposes and set goals;
- independently choose materials, methods, and tasks to advance their learning;
- independently exercise choice in organizing and carrying out the chosen tasks;
- independently choose criteria and methods for evaluation.

Autonomous learners take proactive roles in the learning process, generating ideas and availing themselves of learning opportunities, rather than simply reacting to various opportunities suggested by the instructor.

Interest in the development of autonomous learners in world language instruction has grown significantly in the 21st century. This interest was generated in part by the creation of the European Language Portfolio by the Language Policy Division of the Council of Europe (2001) with its emphasis on learner goal-setting and self-assessment. A second reason for the increased interest in learner autonomy is described by Waschauer (2007): "The exponential growth in the amount and the complexity of information transmitted and shared on the Internet and the capabilities afforded by new information technologies (e.g. hypertext, multimedia, interactivity) result in the continuous emergence of new genres and new literacy practices. The interpretation and understanding of these new genres and practices calls for new models of genre analysis and new approaches to teaching literacy and language where autonomy has to take centre stage."

Little (1991) states that autonomous learners "understand the purpose of their learning programme, explicitly accept responsibility for their learning, share in the setting of learning goals, take initiatives in planning and executing learning activities, and regularly review their learning and evaluate its effectiveness." He continues by identifying three principles that are required in the development of learner autonomy:

- **Involvement** – learners share responsibility for the learning process, including what they will learn and how they will learn it;
- **Reflection** – learners think critically as they plan, monitor, and evaluate their learning;
- **Target language use** – learners use the target language continuously to learn the target language.

The instructor's role in developing autonomous learners is to:

- Establish a classroom where instructor and learners use the target language continuously;
- Involve learners in the selection, analysis, and evaluation of learning activities;
- Help learners set their own learning targets and choose their own learning activities;
- Require learners to identify individual goals but to pursue them through collaborative work;
- Require learners to keep a written record of their learning;
- Engage learners in regular evaluation of their progress as individual learners and as a class.

The following strategies are designed to support and engage learners on their pathways toward independence and autonomy.

STRATEGY: Making personal connections – building self-confidence

Learners are more invested in classes when they feel that the instructor knows them as individuals. When learners are invested, they are more likely to stay on task to complete assigned work, participate in activities, and contribute to class discussions. Instructors demonstrate interest in their learners when they incorporate learners' interests and activities into daily lessons, and when they connect topics to learners' heritage and identity. They take time to talk with learners, give them a website or article they might be interested in that connects their interests to the target language and culture, and select activities that appeal to different talents of the learners. They recognize learners when they make breakthroughs in their ability to understand and communicate in the target language, and are ready to give extra help to learners who are struggling with a concept.

Developing positive relations with learners builds trust and self-confidence. It encourages them to stay focused on understanding the target language even when they may only understand a few key words because they know they won't be left "in the dark." It gives them courage to try to express themselves in the target language even when they may make mistakes or may not know all the words they need to express themselves. Communicating in a new language is taking a risk, and learners need to feel they will not be teased or laughed at for their efforts to communicate. Research shows that establishing positive relationships and respect in the classroom leads to learners trying harder, cooperating more consistently, and helping their classmates (Marzano, 2003). The following are ways to create positive relations and build learner confidence and motivation so they can work independently:

- **Class participation:** Make sure that all learners have the opportunity to participate. Some instructors use index cards with the name of a learner on each card so that the instructor can go through the stack of cards to make sure to call on all learners. Some instructors keep a seating chart on a clipboard where they can quickly mark participation. Both techniques are designed to make sure that no one is forgotten. Recognizing that some learners are hesitant to participate, an instructor can preview a question and tell certain learners to be ready to respond to it.

- **Wait time:** Remember, learners have a lot to process when asked a question. They may have to think about the meaning of the question, and then think of the answer, and then think of how to say the answer in the target language. Those steps take time. When a learner is struggling to answer, think of hints you can give to help the learner retrieve the answer. Hints might include giving a sentence starter, rewording the question into an either/or format or pointing to a poster in the classroom that might contain a helpful word or phrase. You might ask the learner to pair up with someone to think of a response while you expand on the topic of the question, to enrich all learners.
- **Regular individual contacts:** Taking time before class, after class, or when you see learners in the hall to stop and talk is a way to connect with them on a personal level. Using the target language with the learners outside of class enables the learners to build their confidence in responding spontaneously, and to impress others who hear them using the target language. It also sends a message that the target language can be used for more than classwork.
- **Phone calls:** Calling home to tell parents, or telling academic advisors about a learner's positive attitude or cooperative demeanor or helpfulness to other learners, sends a message to both the learner and the parents and advisors that you are aware of the learner's positive contributions to the class atmosphere. That phone call can also serve as a way to find out more about the learner's interests and aspirations. And the call can gain support from the parents or advisors for language learning. These people may have connections to the language through their heritage, travel and living experiences, work, and friends. These connections might lead to guest speakers, field trips, and other resources to enrich the language learning experience.
- **Weekly reflections:** Having learners write weekly reflections is extremely good practice, for several reasons:
  - It is a way for learners to share their feelings, concerns, and questions about class.
  - It is a way for learners to share which activities were helpful to them, which were confusing, and which were not helpful.
  - It is a way for learners to ask questions they might be hesitant to ask in class.
  - It is a way to find out more about the learners in terms of interests and challenges.
  - It gives learners time to compose their thoughts before expressing them in the target language.

If the weekly reflection is set up as a dialogue journal, the instructor can write back to the learner to respond to comments, and to model correct language.

- **Connecting to plans for the future:** It is important that learners see that what they are learning is relevant, connecting not only to their current lives but also to their plans for the future. There are multiple websites that provide reasons for learning a world language, such as ACTFL's LeadwithLanguages.org and Lingholic.com, that highlight not only career options but also personal enrichment reasons for learning another language. All of these resources are helpful, but perhaps the most compelling reasons come from stories from former students who are using their language for work, pleasure, or enrichment. Ask learners to send you a quick note via social media when they use the language they studied or are studying outside of class. Post those responses on a class website or on a bulletin board for others to see. Be sure world languages are represented in campus Job Fairs so learners can see employment opportunities that expect language skills. Those testimonials are motivators for the current class members as they find how graduates are using the language they learned.

STRATEGY: Giving learners choice and control

Offering choices to learners respects learner differences and recognizes that learners have different interests, learning preferences, and readiness levels, and that tasks should be respectful of those factors. In her book, *Learning Through Academic Choice* (2005), Paula Denton suggests giving learners choice in what and how they learn as a powerful tool for motivating learners. She offers four benefits of academic choice:

- Supports learners' intrinsic motivation to learn;
- Encourages learners to learn from each other;
- Draws on different strengths, abilities, and interests;
- Maximizes students' learning.

Choice Boards, a.k.a. Learning Menus, Think-Tac-Toes, and Extension Menus, are an example of giving process and product choice to learners. The Choice Board is set up to vary choices by skills, modality, and interest, all targeted toward a specific learning goal.

In the following sample (Table 13), learners have options for demonstrating learning in the three Modes of Communication related to a unit on movies. Learners pick three tasks, horizontally or diagonally to complete. Note that selecting tasks vertically is not an option, as all three tasks reflect the same mode. The tasks in this sample are intended to build proficiency for Novice Range learners. All three Interpretive tasks are based on authentic texts, and ask the learners to identify the main idea of each text. There are two choices for the Presentational task, one written and one oral. There is also an open space where learners could design a task (with approval from the instructor). The Interpersonal tasks all ask learners to talk about films, either in pairs or small groups or via Skype with learners from a place where the target language is spoken.

Another activity to facilitate choice is called RAFT (Santa, 1988). It helps learners understand what they must consider as they complete a writing assignment so they can ultimately design their own writing assignments. "RAFT"

Table 13. Novice Range Choice Board

Interpretive	Presentational	Interpersonal
Read an advertisement about films currently showing in a theater complex in (X). You and your friends are all able to attend a film running in the afternoon. Which films can you choose? What is the main idea of each film based on the poster showcasing each film?	Make a video clip advertising a favorite film from the United States that you are remaking as a film from (X), using the original film's storyline but making it culturally authentic.	With a partner compare the film listings in a city where the target language is spoken to film listings in your city, noting similarities and differences.
Watch a video clip of a new film in order to determine the kind of film it is (mystery, romance, comedy, drama, animated, etc.) and the main idea of the film.		Within a small group, share your favorite film of all the films you have seen, briefly explaining the plot for the film and why it is the best film you have ever seen.
Listen to a famous actor describe his or her new film during an interview in order to identify the main idea of the film and the role that the actor plays.	Write a review of a film, giving the main idea of the story, the quality of performance of the actors, and how many stars, out of 5, the film merits.	Skype with a sister school/university where the target language is spoken to share favorite films and actors, and why they like them.

Table 14. RAFT for Novice learners about shopping

Role	You will assume the role of: *Department store worker*
Audience	The audience is: *Customers in the community*
Format	The format is: *Advertising flyer*
Topic	The topic: *Clothing sale*
Completed Task:	

stands for Role, Audience, Format, and Topic. First, the learners need to decide what their role is as a writer. Next, they need to determine the audience that will read their work. Then, they need to consider the format required for the task. Finally, they need to think about what the topic should be. When instructors introduce the RAFT activity to learners, it is helpful to give them a template with the choices pre-selected. Table 14 is a sample pre-selected RAFT for Novice learners in a unit about shopping.

After the learners have practiced using RAFT and are comfortable with how the four elements influence their writing, the instructor can give them a grid with options for each component. Learners choose their Role, Audience, Format, and Topic from the grid. Table 15 is a sample RAFT with options related to eating in a restaurant for learners at the Intermediate proficiency level.

Table 15. RAFT chart of options for an Intermediate task

Role of the Writer	Audience	Format	Topic
Chef	Cooks	Restaurant review	Why the restaurant is a good choice
Diner	Friends and family	Menu	Best foods to eat in a certain city
Travel writer	Nutritionist	Travel blog	Healthy food choices
Food Critic	Tourists	Travel guidebook	Unusual dining experience

Table 16 is another RAFT completed by a group of Mandarin instructors. Notice that the role of the writer is either an animal or an object associated with the Chinese New Year, sparking the learners' imagination and including culture.

Table 16. RAFT for Mandarin learners about Chinese New Year

Role of the Writer	Audience	Format	Topic
Year monster	Children	Script	Why can't I scare people anymore?
Zodiac animals	Cat	News report	Why didn't you get chosen?
Firecracker	Visitors	Invitation	Inviting people to a Chinese New Year celebration
Red envelope	Self	Diary/journal entry	How am I going to spend my money?
Dumpling	Dumpling maker	Blog post	Can we change the dumpling recipe?

After the learners have successfully completed several RAFT writing assignments, they may choose their RAFT elements on their own for certain assignments. Table 17 is a chart with a few examples for each category to help spark learners' creativity:

Table 17. Options for each category of a RAFT assignment

Role of the Writer	Audience	Format	Topic
Artist Explorer Reporter Parent President Inventor Musician Author Designer Athlete Scientist Salesperson Pilot Actor	General public Committee Classmates Community members State government Sports enthusiasts Instructors Parents Teenagers College students Tourists Concert goers Museum visitors Children	Journal Editorial Brochure Interview Cartoon Critique Bio sketch Newspaper article Blog Website Letter Invitation Advertisement Script	Environment Travel destinations Cuisine Art Music Theatre Movies Novels, short stories Sports Current events Cities Celebrations Social media Famous people

Giving learners a template (Table 18) to complete reminds them to address all four elements in RAFT.

Table 18. RAFT template

Role:	Audience:
Format:	**Topic:**
Completed Task:	

STRATEGY: Creating learning centers

Learning centers enable learners to work independently at their own pace within the classroom. Setting up permanent learning centers around the classroom is helpful for both the instructor and learners. Learners can go to a learning center either as part of a class session, as an assignment in the Language Learning Center, or when they have free time. In all cases, the learners interact with the content in a variety of ways through a range of modalities. Each learning center includes a card or sign with brief, clearly written instructions to the learners about what to do at the center so they can begin their work independently. Instructions written in the target language and in English make the station accessible to all learners. Gradually the English instructions can be eliminated as the learners become knowledgeable about the purpose for each center. Ideally, all learners complete all learning centers at some point during the unit of instruction, letting them practice different ways of learning. One framework for creating permanent learning centers is shown below in Table 19. This framework shows nine different centers; however, the instructor can set up centers as space allows. It is possible to combine two modalities into one center or rotate the modalities in and out of the centers. University instructors who teach on-line courses can choose the modalities that best fit the form of instruction.

When implementing learning centers in the classroom or a Language Learning Center, consider the following:

- Space limitations in the classroom or teaching situation;
- Routines and procedures for using the learning centers;
- Purpose for using learning centers as part of a unit of instruction;
- Amount of class time devoted to learning center work;
- Expectations to complete all or a certain number of learning centers;
- Evaluation of work in each center.

To ensure accountability for completing the activities at each center, give learners a folder where they can place work for each center they complete. It is helpful to include a "map" of the centers so learners can check off the center as they complete the activity. On-line instructors can have learners email their products or post them on the course management system.

Table 19. Framework for Learning Centers

Speaking Center Look at a photo or drawing of a scene from the target culture. Record your response to: What do you see?	**Listening Center** Listen to a song or podcast or an audiobook, and respond by circling words/ideas that reflect the content, or answer comprehension questions, or draw a picture that captures the main idea of the recording.	**Writing Center** Respond in writing to written, visual, or audio prompt. Using a word bank with new vocabulary can be part of the prompt.
Reading Center Read brochures, magazine articles, flyers, stories, and comic books, and complete a task based on the content of the authentic text.	**Technology Center** Play online games to practice vocabulary, language functions and related structures. Take virtual tours of places in the countries where the target language is spoken.	**Creative Center** Create a drawing, model, or authentic craft.
Hands-on Center Place sentence strips in a logical order to create a story. Match cards that have either the first half of a sentence or the second half of a sentence to make a complete sentence.	**Act-it-out Center** Act out vocabulary or expressions for a partner to guess.	**Instructor Center** Instructor works with a learner to deepen understanding, fill in learning gaps, or extend their learning.

After the required number of centers is completed, the learners submit their folders to the instructor for review, feedback, and credit for the work completed.

STRATEGY: Providing challenging, but achievable tasks that emphasize higher order thinking skills

Tasks are more engaging when learners are required to think at higher levels and are expected to go beyond merely demonstrating understanding of the content. Learners' thinking is extended beyond the remembering and understanding levels to applying what they learned to new contexts, analyzing and evaluating information they read, hear or view, and ultimately creating new understandings. Once again, sentence frames and word banks can help Novice language learners express their ideas. For example, second graders in a German FLES classroom completed a unit on animals. They created an imaginary animal and described it with a sentence frame as a basis for their explanation: "This is a (name of animal). It lives in (the mountains, the desert, the ocean, etc.) I like it because it is (adjective) and it is not (adjective)."

Instructors who are attuned to learners' readiness to approach a task can customize the task in four ways (Tomlinson & Allan, 2000), and still maintain the challenge of higher order thinking:

- **Vary the degree of independence in completing a task:** For example, rather than assigning the task of making a comic book based on the biography of a famous person from the target culture and giving no further guidance, the instructor could break the task into steps, explaining the steps one at a time so learners are not overwhelmed.
- **Vary the specificity of instructions:** If an important goal for the task is to encourage creativity and imagination, the instructor might limit the number of details in the instructions. For example, learners may be asked to create a children's story that includes cultural products and practices from the Portuguese-speaking world. No other expectations are given, except to make it a "best-seller."
- **Vary the degree of structure:** The instructor can tell learners to create graphic organizers to summarize an article they read, or the instructor can give the learners a specific graphic organizer to use with a sample entry of the graphic organizer to model how to complete it.
- **Reteach a specific pattern or concept in small groups:** The instructor might create groups where two or three learners who understand the pattern or concept teach two or three who don't understand how to use it. Or the instructor might work with a small group of learners who are having difficulty understanding a pattern or concept while the rest of the class works on an application task.

Tiered assignments are examples of respectful tasks where learners work on different levels of activities, all with the same essential understanding or goal in mind (Williams, 2002). Instructors create tiered activities when differences exist in readiness among learners. To create tiered activities, first determine the task for the mid-level learners. Next, design activities for struggling learners with scaffolds such as word banks and step-by-step procedures. Finally, design activities for advanced learners. As illustrated in the example that follows (Table 20), the tiered activity provides parallel tasks at varying degrees of complexity, and with varying degrees of scaffolding, all with the same learning goals.

Table 20. Example of tiered assignments

Tier A	Tier B	Tier C
Learners read an article about environmental awareness with key vocabulary highlighted and linked to illustrations. Next, they compare and contrast their town with the one described in the article using a Venn diagram with each section labeled, and an example in each section.	Learners read an article about environmental awareness. Next, they compare and contrast their town with the one in the article using a Venn diagram.	Learners read an article about environmental awareness. Next, they compare and contrast their town with the one in the article by creating their own graphic organizer.

STRATEGY: Providing time for reflection

Learners benefit from quiet time to think about what they have just learned, work they have just completed, feelings they have about what and how they are learning, or how they can apply what they've learned beyond the current unit of study. Preparing learners for reflection means signaling that it is time to look back rather than forward for a moment. The primary focus is on what they have learned from an activity, lesson, or unit. It is important to establish from the beginning that reflection has to start in the target language. For beginning learners in the early weeks, it might mean drawing and labeling a picture as a starting point for their reflection. Once they have exhausted what they can say in the target language, they can finish their reflection in English. Let learners know that the more they write in the target language, the more they will be able to write. Their reflection journal is a way to visually show the progress they are making in expressing themselves in the target language. At the beginning of the year, what they can write in the target language might be words, phrases, or simple sentences. By the end of the semester or year, the number of sentences has increased, and the sentences may be longer, containing more details. Sentence stems can also help learners express their thoughts in the target language. Here are some examples:

- I liked this project because...
- I learned that...
- I want to learn more about....

Another way to encourage reflection is to give learners a prompt, such as:

- Write a letter to yourself detailing what you learned from (a story, an activity, etc).
- What advice would you give yourself before starting the next unit?

> IDEA-SHARING
> Getting to know the learners in your classes is extremely important for successful learning. Share ideas on how you learn about learners' interests and how they learn best at the beginning of the school year.

Strategies to Facilitate Cooperation and Collaboration Among Learners

As stated earlier, being an independent or autonomous learner doesn't mean the learner is always working alone. The following strategies emphasize cooperation and teamwork.

STRATEGY: Forming a community of learners

Working together toward common goals: The members of a class must feel they are working together to make progress towards greater proficiency, and they can all help each other make progress. Keep a large poster of the NCSSFL-ACTFL Can-Do Proficiency Benchmarks displayed in the classroom, or create your own visual of progress toward greater proficiency. Periodically show the class where they are on the chart. Because it takes time to progress, consider subdividing the boxes for each level of proficiency so you can mark progress through a level. Some instructors use a world map and set communication and culture goals that connect to an itinerary through the countries where the language is spoken.

Building Community Through Music: Music appeals to nearly, if not all, learners, and can unify elements of the world language class. Calm music can settle a rowdy class. Lively music can wake up a lethargic class. Music can set the mood as learners walk into class, carrying them to another place, and maybe another time in history. Through music, learners find out about history, current events, celebrations, and other cultural topics.

Table 21. Connecting music to the three modes of communication

	Novice	Intermediate	Advanced
Interpretive Mode	Act out the words to a song or create gestures to accompany a favorite song from the target culture	Listen to a song from the target culture to identify the main idea of the song, and some lyrics that support the main idea	Read an article about a songwriter or performer, and identify his/her inspiration for a song and the message he/she is trying to convey. Evaluate how effectively the songwriter conveyed the intended message
Interpersonal Mode	Exchange opinions with a classmate about favorite songs and/or musicians from the target culture	Skype with a classroom where the target language is spoken to share opinions about various types of music and songs	Exchange information and opinions with a partner to be ready to present one side in a debate on which is more stronger: the influence of American music on music in the target culture or the influence of music from the target culture on American music.
Presentational Mode	Create a new verse for a favorite song from the target culture, using the patterns from other verses	Write a review of a song, including background on the artist and composer	Create a presentation to share the life and works of a musician from the target culture who made a lasting contribution to the music world

Music can signal transitions in a lesson: "When you hear the music stop, it's time to return to your desks."

In "Language Can be Music to Students' Ears" (The Language Educator 2011), Patricia Koning points out that music can reinforce vocabulary and grammar, especially if certain words or patterns are repeated several times within a song. Raps, chants, and cheers are especially effective in terms of repetition. There is something magical about music, because learners don't seem to mind singing a song more than once. And with that repetition, the patterns and vocabulary get planted in learners' brains, increasing their fluency in the target language. Add gestures and movement to a song or rap, and the words will stay with the learners forever!

Table 21 gives some examples of tasks based on music from the target culture for the three modes of communication.

Integrating movement into daily lessons: In Eric Jensen's book, *Teaching with the Brain in Mind* (2005), the author cites "strong evidence that supports the connection between movement and learning." Giving learners opportunities to get up out of their seats to interact with classmates strengthens learning and builds community. Movement increases the amount of oxygen in the blood, increasing attention, concentration, and memory. Movement allows learners to talk with several people instead of just the person sitting nearby. Here are some other ways to add movement to language practice:

- **Human graphs:** Learners line up based on their responses to a prompt in order to create a human bar graph. For example, learners line up by the month of their birth, or they line up by the number of hours they watch TV each day. After counting and recording the responses on the board, learners can return to their seats to write their findings, make comparisons, or write opinions, depending on the language level of the learners. For example, a beginning language learner might write: Six people have birthdays in January. An intermediate learner might write: There are fewer birthdays in March than in April. The fewest birthdays are in August. A more advanced learner might write: It is too bad that so many people have birthdays in the summer because...
- **Letter pop-up:** Learners are assigned a letter of the alphabet. The instructor calls out a vocabulary word. Learners "pop up" out of their seats and say the letter, using correct pronunciation in the target language when their letter occurs in the word. If the letters are written on cards or paper plates, the learners could come to the front of the room to spell out the word.
- **Opinion continuum:** Learners stand along an imaginary line to indicate to what degree they agree or disagree with a statement. Then they form pairs or small groups of people of similar opinions to say why they agree, are neutral, or disagree. Finally a pair or small group finds a group that is not of the same opinion, and discuss why their opinions differ.
- **Quote pairs:** Each learner is given a card with either the first half or the second half of a quote. They must walk around and find the other half of the quote. Afterward, they create a conversation where the quote could be used and share their conversation with the class.
- **Energizers:** After a session focused on reading or writing, have learners get out of their seats to play a game called "Touch blue but not on you." The learners listen to the instructor describe what they need to find and touch in the classroom. The instructor might say: "Touch something green" or "Touch something round." This serves as a quick 30-second activity to get everyone moving, and to review some basic vocabulary.
- **Gallery Walks:** Pairs of learners read different articles and create a drawing that captures the main idea of the article. They post their drawings on the walls of the classroom. Then all learners rotate around the room to view the drawings and discuss with their partner what they think is the main idea of the article.
- **Chalk Talks:** Photos of different places in the target culture are posted on the walls. Learners write their impressions of the photos on Post-it notes to attach to the walls next to the photos. Others can add comments to the Post-it notes already in place or add new Post-it notes.

STRATEGY: Collaborating with others

The Partnership for 21st Century Skills (www.P21.org) identifies collaboration as a necessary skill for success in work and life in the 21st century. Learners who have experience collaborating on tasks and projects:

- Demonstrate the ability to work effectively and respectfully with diverse teams;
- Exercise flexibility and willingness to help make necessary compromises to accomplish a common goal;
- Assume shared responsibility for collaborative work, and value the individual contributions made by each team member.

A distinction between collaboration and cooperation was prevalent in the 1990s. Today the distinction is fading, and some education literature uses the two terms interchangeably. Marzano (2010) identifies cooperative learning as one of the nine most effective instructional strategies available to classroom instructors. His research shows that learners working in groups attain higher levels of thinking and retain information for longer periods of time than learners who work alone. The opportunity to work together in pairs and small groups on a task gives learners a purpose to communicate. While collaborative groups are generally formed to work on a project that requires more than one class period, pairs and small groups can be used daily for a variety of activities. Here are some ways to group learners:

- **Folded Line:** Learners line up based on a selected characteristic (birthday, first letter of their name, number of years they have lived in the community, etc.). The line is folded in the center to form two lines. Learners partner with the classmate across from them.
- **Commonalities:** Learners group themselves based on something they have in common: wear glasses/contacts, same birth month, favorite color, etc.
- **Grouping cards, sticks:** Learners receive a stick or card with a symbol on it and group accordingly.
- **Clock/compass/map partners:** Learners make appointments with their classmates for each hour on the clock, each direction on the compass, or each city on the map of a country where the target language is spoken.

The following guidelines contribute to the success of collaborative or cooperative group work. These guidelines are especially useful when groups are going to work together on an extended project:

- **Keep the group size to four.** Even numbers of group members facilitates breaking the group into pairs to discuss the task. Equal numbers of females and males in a group increases the cooperation among the group members. It is also helpful to make sure the group members represent a variety of talents. For example, one person may be especially good at design, one may be a musician, one may be good at organizing tasks.
- **Establish group goals and individual accountability.** Everyone takes responsibility for the successful completion of the task or project and is held accountable for their portion of the work and the learning that results.
- **Establish group norms to build trust and ensure open communication.** For longer projects, groups often create and sign a contract outlining agreed-upon behaviors for working in the group. For example: how to take turns to talk, how to disagree respectfully, how to move the discussion forward or return the discussion to the topic, when to request outside intervention from the instructor.
- **Ensure that each member of the group does equal work and contributes important information to shape the final product.** By dividing up important work, group members realize they can have a successful final product only if they work together. Use two rubrics: one that assesses individual work, and one that assesses group work.
- **Consider using a pre- and post-test to provide evidence of learning.** This can be a written response identifying the background knowledge learners bring to the task, and a reflection at the end of the task about what the learners know now that they didn't know before.
- **Provide ongoing feedback to the process and content, and ask groups to self-assess during and at the end of the task.** Continually assess the quality and effectiveness of group interactions. Each member is responsible for evaluating his or her own contributions as well as those of others.

STRATEGY: Building authentic communication through games

Lee Su Kim, in her article "Creative Games for the Language Class" (1995), suggests the following advantages for designing carefully structured "gaming" activities. Games....

- Provide a welcome break from the usual routine of the language class;
- Are motivating and challenging;
- Help learners sustain the energy for learning;
- Provide language practice in speaking, writing, listening, and reading;
- Encourage learners to interact spontaneously with each other;
- Create a meaningful context for language use.

When selecting a game, instructors need to consider its value as a tool for learning. These questions, whose key words spell out the word "PLAY," provide a set of criteria to use to analyze the value of including a game in daily instruction:

- P – Does the **Purpose** of the game relate to the unit goals?
- L – Are the **Language** skills being practiced the skills learners need at this point in the unit?

- **A** – How does the activity **Advance** students' learning?
- **Y** – Will the activity **Yield** any information about the learners' understanding and use of the target language?

There are several stipulations to using games effectively in the world language classroom. Rodney Tyson (1998), in his article "Serious Fun: Using Games, Jokes, and Stories in the Language Classroom," suggests that games should have more value than fun. In *Keys to Planning for Learning* (2013), Clementi & Terrill submit that "games cannot be played in isolation and need to be connected to other learning activities." Robert Marzano (2010), in his article "Using Games to Enhance Student Achievement," encourages instructors to get the most out of classroom games by making sure to debrief the game after it is completed to highlight what has been learned. As Tyson's guidelines suggested, games should not be too complicated. One way to minimize the amount of class time dedicated to explanations and rules is to choose games learners have already played in their L1. Providing a word bank (Figure 22) of game-related vocabulary helps learners successfully stay in the target language while playing the game.

Figure 22. Word bank to facilitate staying in the target language during a game

Word bank for games

Whose turn is it?
It's your (my) turn.
Roll the dice.
Move your player (forward, backwards) x spaces.
Shuffle the cards.
Pick a card.
How many points do you have?
Who is winning?

STRATEGY: Organizing and implementing project-based learning

The premise for project-based learning is learners working on teams to complete significant long-term projects based on an essential question about a real-world issue. The emphasis is on active, learner-directed explorations of an issue that is personally meaningful. Relevance is a critical characteristic, giving learners choice and voice in the entire learning experience. Ultimately the learners share their creative solutions to an identified issue with audiences beyond the classroom. Larmer & Mergendoller (2007) list seven essentials for project-based learning based on their work at the Buck Institute for Education:

- **A need to know:** To engage the learners and initiate questions, think of how to grab their attention. Powerful images or a short well-crafted video may achieve this goal. Another possibility is to share a news article or clip or short story about the issue or topic you plan to explore.
- **An essential question:** A good question is open-ended and brings the topic or issue into focus.
- **Learner voice and choice:** Share components for the project and let learners select which components they want to explore. The instructor may need to offer guided choice, asking learners to select an option in each of two or three categories, and then requiring all learners to complete certain components.
- **21st-Century Skills:** The project is strengthened by the inclusion of opportunities for collaboration, critical thinking, and creativity.
- **Inquiry and Innovation:** With a good question, learners are motivated to find a new answer, a new product.
- **Feedback and Revision:** Learners need to give and receive feedback from their classmates on the tasks they are completing as part of the process of creating a high-quality final product. They need opportunities to reflect on their work and the work of the class periodically, describing what they have learned so far and new questions they need to explore related to their findings.
- **Publicly Presented Product:** Learners need to share their final products with an audience beyond the classroom.

The standards-based Integrated Performance Assessment unit framework works well as a framework for project-based learning in the world language classroom. One way to initiate a project-based learning instructional unit is to connect with The Peace Corps World Wise Schools (www.peacecorps.gov/educators). One of their initiatives is "Thinking Outside the Envelope," connecting Peace Corps volunteers around the world with classrooms in the United States with suggestions for projects where learners can go beyond a pen pal exchange. The Peace Corps volunteers also review and accept suggestions for other creative ways to connect classrooms with the communities where they live and work.

STRATEGY: Working together during hands-on activities

Hands-on activities personally involve learners in doing something to gain knowledge and/or skills. Hands-on activities are especially useful in learning about the people and cultures who speak the target language. It is truly learning by doing. Learners are learning the target language by actually using it as they learn how to play an authentic sport or game, to learn how to make a food or craft, or learn a dance.

Hands-on activities also include performing scenes from films, plays, novels, or television shows from the target cultures. For example, learners in a French class presented scenes from *Le Bal des Voleurs* (The Robbers' Ball) by Anouilh. They researched background information about the time period, the author, and the significance of the play in France and globally. In preparing to present the play, learners searched for appropriate props and costumes and scenery that reflected the time period and culture. They memorized lines and practiced saying them with correct pronunciation, intonation, and emotion, requiring them to understand both the literal and inferential levels of what they are saying. They determined how the actors would move around on stage, and what gestures and facial expressions they would use. They designed a program that included background information about the play, and short biographies of the actors. The final performance for an audience that included other French classes, parents, faculty members, and other interested people was the culmination of all the preparation described above. Learners were extremely proud of their performance, as was the audience. Projects like this one are ideal topics to reflect upon for college application forms often required for college entrance. Additionally, university students can reflect on similar projects as they seek employment after graduation.

In the 21st century, technology is a key tool for engagement and collaboration. For example, advances in technology has introduced the Maker Movement:

> The learning that occurs through the experience of making and the learning that occurs through instruction in new media share an unexpected pedagogical kinship. As Groff (2013) points out, we are reaching a period where it is just as easy for young people to produce...multimodal, multimedia content as to consume it" (p. 23). Similarly, the phenomenon that some have termed the "maker movement," which describes the wave of interest in constructing and sharing personal inventions and creative artifacts, reconfigures the learner as a *producer* rather than a consumer. Makers—operating in schools and museums, in libraries and community centers, in homes and specially designed makerspaces—contend that the process of imagining, creating, refining, and sharing a custom artifact offers a unique form of both collaborative and self-directed learning for youth and adults alike.
>
> (*Harvard Educational Review*, Winter 2014)

What does the Maker Movement mean for world languages? In classrooms where learners use the target language to respond to an essential question, they might create a digital or physical artifact to answer the question or solve the problem identified in the essential question, and then share what they have created with a local or global audience. For example, in a standards-based thematic unit based on the essential question "Does clothing tell a story?," learners might digitally create an outfit that reflects someone's heritage or interests or that is environmentally friendly. Earlier in this chapter, the discussion of "hands-on" learning included an example where learners performed a French play. For this project, learners could have used a 3D printer to create authentic props for the play. The possibilities are endless.

Summary: World language instructors and their classrooms are often among the most animated and interactive in their school or university. The key to engaging learners in the world language classroom is to make them active participants in the learning process where lesson activities are "hands-on" and "minds-on." Making real life connections, giving learners choice and control, providing challenging but achievable tasks, allowing for collaboration, and incorporating higher order thinking all contribute to learner engagement for learners of all ages and all levels of language ability.

Reflect on the essential question: How do the strategies I choose encourage learner engagement?

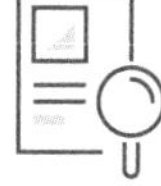

Analyze an example of activities that have been adapted to increase learner engagement.

Examine the following activities and their adaptations. Using the Engagement Checklist, evaluate how the adapted activity increases learner engagement.

Activity	Adapted Activity to Increase Learner Engagement	Engagement Checklist
For a unit on housing, learners complete a handout where they answer comprehension questions about sample real estate ads.	Learners go online and search for housing in a city in the target culture using authentic real estate sites in the target language. They collect information on a graphic organizer. In the end, through a presentational writing task, learners decide which option they would choose for a stay in the city and tell why.	☐ Making real-life connections ☐ Giving learners choice and control ☐ Providing challenging but achievable tasks ☐ Allowing for collaboration ☐ Providing experiential, hands-on tasks ☐ Incorporating higher-order thinking
The instructor creates a Jeopardy game containing clues about a story that was read by the class. The game is conducted in a whole class format where the class is divided into two teams and individual team members give responses to earn points for their team.	As a homework assignment, small groups of learners collaboratively create an online Jeopardy game using the Jeopardy Labs website (jeopardylabs.com) on the topic of a story that was read by the class. The following class day, all learners play their classmates' versions of the game simultaneously in small groups.	☐ Making real-life connections ☐ Giving learners choice and control ☐ Providing challenging but achievable tasks ☐ Allowing for collaboration ☐ Providing experiential, hands-on tasks ☐ Incorporating higher-order thinking
The instructor gives the class an article about current events in a country where the target language is spoken. Learners read the article and answer comprehension questions individually.	The instructor gives pairs of learners different front pages of newspapers from countries where the target language is spoken. Pairs note the headlines on the front page, noting if the news is local, national, or international, and the theme of the news article (politics, sports, entertainment, etc). Learners then form a group of four to compare the news from their front pages, noting similarities and differences. Next, learners create groups of eight and compare their front pages, creating a visual to illustrate the range of topics in the newspapers they reviewed.	☐ Making real-life connections ☐ Giving learners choice and control ☐ Providing challenging but achievable tasks ☐ Allowing for collaboration ☐ Providing experiential, hands-on tasks ☐ Incorporating higher-order thinking

Apply ideas to your practice using the knowledge gained from the chapter: Think about an activity you recently implemented in your classroom.

How might you adapt the activity to increase learner engagement? Use the characteristics from the Engagement Checklist to evaluate the adapted activity's level of learner engagement:

- Implement the activity.
- Collect data in the evidence column, and reflect on changes you see in the level of learner engagement in the revised activity.

Activity:	Adaptation:
Student engagement	Evidence
☐ Making real-life connections ☐ Giving learners choice and control ☐ Providing challenging but achievable tasks ☐ Allowing for collaboration ☐ Providing experiential, hands-on tasks ☐ Incorporating higher-order thinking	

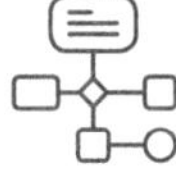

Extend your learning by completing these activities.

1. Think about a game you recently incorporated into your classroom. Reflect on how that experience measured up to the four 'PLAY" analysis questions. What enhancements will you make to the game next time?

> - **P** - Does the **Purpose** of the game relate to the unit goals?
> - **L** - Are the **Language** skills being practiced the skills learners need at this point in the unit?
> - **A** - How does the activity **Advance** students' learning?
> - **Y** - Will the activity **Yield** any information about the learners' understanding and use of the target language?

2. Videotape a lesson with the goal of analyzing the levels of learner engagement. Determine the degree to which all learners were actively engaged in the lesson.
3. Create and administer a survey to collect data about the types of classroom activities learners find most engaging and helpful to their learning.
4. Collect data on how music influences learners in terms of mood and engagement.
5. Review a series of lessons. Which instructional strategies within the lessons were the most engaging for your learners? Explore the reasons why.

Deepen your knowledge by exploring additional resources.

Buck Institute for Education Project-based Learning, http://www.bie.org/

Halverson, E. R., & Sheridan, K. M. (2014). *The Maker Movement in education*. Harvard Educational Review, *Winter 2014*.

Jensen, E. (2008). *Brain-based learning: The new paradigm of teaching.* Thousand Oaks, CA: Corwin Press.

Martinez, S., & Stager G. (2013). *Invent to learn: Making, tinkering, and engineering in the classroom*. Los Angeles, CA: Constructing Modern Knowledge Press.

The High School Survey of Student Engagement (http://ceep.indiana.edu/about/additional.html).

The Maine Center for Meaningful and Engaged Learning (http://www.mcmel.org/).

The National Survey on Student Engagement (http://nsse.indiana.edu).

The Schlechty Center (http://www.schlechtycenter.org/).

Sousa, D. A., & Tomlinson, C. A. (2011). *Differentiation and the brain: How neuroscience supports the learner-friendly classroom.* Bloomington, IN: Solution Tree Press.

Chapter 5 | Evaluating Instructional Strategies

How do I evaluate the effectiveness of the strategies I use?

- Focus on the Structure of a Lesson Plan
- Focus on Learner Engagement
- Using Learner Feedback to Evaluate Instructional Strategies
- Final Thoughts

"By studying Latin, I like to think that my students learn how to think logically and critically, act rationally, and argue persuasively, even if they do not realize it and cannot articulate it until long after they no longer remember conjugations or demonstrative adjectives. They will have immersed themselves in a language and culture through which they were compelled to reexamine their own values and beliefs. As a result, they come to be scholars and lifelong learners, to lead informed lives, to respect knowledge for its own sake, to go beyond a shallow understanding of the world, and to seek the truth—for only then can we come to recognize what is good and beautiful when we see it, and even fight for it when we have to."

—Edward Zarrow, ACTFL Teacher of the Year 2016

Edward Zarrow, ACTFL 2016 National Teacher of the Year, very eloquently expressed the goals of all instructors in his statement introducing this chapter. The language instruction strategies in this publication are intended to give instructors some of the tools needed to effectively teach toward those goals. Let's look more carefully at the topic of this chapter: evaluation.

Taking time to assess the effectiveness of instructional strategies yields many benefits for informing future lesson-planning decisions that will in turn influence how well learners understand and communicate in the language they are learning.

The National Board for Professional Teaching Standards (NBPTS) includes instructor reflection as one of its nine standards. Standard VIII describes the actions of accomplished educators who reflect as practitioners who "critically examine their practice on a regular basis by describing, analyzing, and reflecting on their successes as well as on their setbacks in the classroom, rethinking instructional choices to maximize student learning, and fulfill short- and long-term objectives."

Focus on the Structure of a Lesson Plan

Evaluating the effectiveness of instructional strategies for a single lesson begins with reflection about the lesson plan itself. Some instructors may keep a reflective journal where they record their thoughts about the effectiveness of the lesson. Others may write notes on their daily lesson plans, including any reminders of what to do differently the next time they teach the lesson. Table 22 (see p. 72) includes questions to consider after teaching a lesson.

Table 22. Reflection questions to consider after teaching a lesson

Aspect of the Lesson	Possible questions
Structure of the lesson	• Was the pace of the lesson appropriate? • Did the choice of lesson activities move learners toward the learning targets? • What percentage of the lesson was teacher-centered, and what percentage was learner-centered?
Content of the lesson	• Which Modes of Communication were practiced? • How was culture represented in the lesson? • Were the lesson activities appropriate for the language abilities of my learners? • How did I use what I know about my learners to guide the lesson?
Instructor actions	• What did I do to engage learners who were not participating? • How did I differentiate instruction to meet the needs of all learners in my class? • How did I monitor learners while they completed activities? What sort of feedback did I give them?
Learner actions	• Which activities seemed to engage the learners? • What did I notice about how the learners interacted with each other?
Effectiveness of lesson	• What evidence did I collect about student learning? • How would I evaluate the lesson?
Future implications	• What would I do differently next time I teach this lesson? • Based on this lesson, what do I have to do tomorrow and beyond?

Another tool for reflecting on the effectiveness of a lesson was created by Peter Pappas (2010). His "Taxonomy of Reflection" (Figure 23) invites instructors to align their reflections on their teaching with the various levels of Bloom's Taxonomy. Begin at the bottom of the taxonomy and think about the components of the lesson you taught. Continue up the taxonomy, pausing to respond to each question. You may want to record your responses in a personal journal.

Figure 23. Taxonomy of Reflection by Pappas

The following questions represent another way for instructors to reflect on daily lesson plans:

- How does my lesson plan allow each learner to engage in the learning?

Discussion: As instructors plan their lessons with active learner engagement in mind, the goal is to select lesson activities where learners are offered frequent and varied opportunities to practice language skills. Traditional practices, such as calling on individuals to respond to questions asked by the instructor, limit the opportunities for all learners to participate actively. All learners can be engaged simultaneously if instructors use, for example, inside-outside circles where learners in the inside circle face the learners in the outside circle. The instructor displays a question for learners to ask, or asks learners to generate questions about a topic. The learners discuss the prompt. After 30 seconds, the learners all slide one person to the right. With a new partner, the learners discuss the same prompt, or the instructor can introduce a new prompt. This type of activity maximizes talk time for the learners and allows the instructor to listen to how well they are using the target language.

- How can I ensure that every learner has practiced all three Modes of Communication (Interpersonal, Interpretive, and Presentational) during the lesson?

Discussion: During lesson planning, the instructor needs to continuously refer to the unit goals and summative assessments for the unit, and then identify how the day's lesson connects to those goals and assessments. It is optimal to structure a lesson that integrates all three Modes of Communication. For example, pairs or small groups of learners read different articles related to the unit theme, and fill in a graphic organizer to pull out the main idea and supporting details (Interpretive Mode). Next, new groups are formed, with each person in the new group sharing the article he or she read. After all articles have been shared, the group discusses what the articles have in common and what content is unique (Interpersonal Mode). Finally, the group works together to create a summary of the information in the articles (Presentational Mode).

- Is there a quick way to check for understanding to verify that the lesson plan objectives were met?

Discussion: Formative assessments can be completed using Every Pupil Response (EPR) strategies. These strategies give instructors immediate feedback on where learners are in their learning. Through EPR activities, learners' responses reveal gaps in their learning, misconceptions they hold, and verify what they know and are able to do. Some examples include:

    - **Pinch cards:** Learners point to an expression or visual on an index card (Figure 24) to indicate their response to a question posed by the instructor. The instructor may show three possible answers (e.g., A/B/C) and learners identify their answer by pinching that answer (e.g., B) between their thumb and forefinger and holding up the card for the instructor to see which response each learner pinched. The card might have different options on the back side (e.g., True/False/Not sure). In another example, during a unit on health, learners are given scenarios, some logical, some illogical (e.g. "She is coughing because her foot hurts."). Learners indicate if they agree or not with the statement by pinching on the pinch card "yes," "no" or "not sure" (written in the target language) to indicate their responses.

Figure 24: Pinch card

A	**Yes**
B	**No**
C	**Not sure**

    - **Thumbs up, thumbs down:** After the instructor introduces a new concept or gives instructions for an activity, learners indicate their understanding by gesturing with a thumb up for understanding, a thumb sideways if understanding is not complete, and a thumb down if they do not understand.
    - **Whiteboards:** Dry erase boards are used by learners individually or in small groups to display their responses to instructor prompts. After viewing a video clip about environmental issues, for example, the instructor asks comprehension and extension questions about the clip. Learners, in small groups, collaborate about their answers and, when given the signal, display their responses on their whiteboards. Mini whiteboards are available commercially from several teacher supply stores or can be made from whiteboard materials found at larger hardware outlets.
    - **Signal cards:** Learners use cards to signal their understanding: red indicates low understanding, yellow indicates partial understanding, and green indicates complete understanding. After viewing an advertisement from the target culture, for example, learners indicate their understanding using the signal cards. Based on the learner responses, the instructor determines if showing the advertisement a second time is needed.
    - **Fist to Five:** Learners indicate their level of understanding using their fingers. A closed fist indicates no understanding, three fingers, some understanding, and five fingers, complete understanding. The instructor, for instance, has learners examine an infographic about interviewing for jobs in the target culture. After analyzing the infographic, learners indicate their level of understanding using the fist or five strategy. Based on the learner responses, the instructor may ask learners to work in partners or small groups to further unlock the text.

IDEA-SHARING
There are many lesson plan templates available to instructors.
When writing a lesson plan, which elements are most important to ensure the lesson is well-organized and learner-centered?

Focus on Learner Engagement

In the process of planning lessons, there are several factors to consider. The factors, discussed below, are drawn from multiple sources on learner engagement, such as the National Survey on Student Engagement, which is administered to college-aged students, and the High School Survey of Student Engagement developed by the Center for Evaluation and Education Policy at Indiana University, Bloomington. The list provided is not all-inclusive and does not imply that a single activity should include all of the characteristics to qualify as "engaging." Factors important for creating engaging instructional activities include:

- *Making sure the purpose for an activity or assignment is clear.* When learners understand why they are doing an activity or assignment and how it will help them learn to communicate in the target language, they are much more likely to actively participate. When they understand the instructions for an activity or assignment, they won't complete the work incorrectly or fail to complete the work.
- *Making real-life connections.* Topics and tasks that connect to learners' interests and their curiosity about the world increase motivation. Sharing a wide variety of authentic print, oral, and visual texts with learners sends a message that the language they are learning is vital.
- *Giving learners choice and control.* When learners are offered choices in products, performances, and other classroom structures, it empowers them to become more actively engaged in the learning. Opportunities for learner self-assessment through rubrics and checklists give control to students over their success.
- *Providing challenging but achievable tasks.* Tasks that are challenging but achievable are motivating and engaging to learners, encourage perseverance, and build confidence in language learners. Include tasks where learners are asked to make predictions based on what they have read or viewed. Let them play with ideas to come up with a novel solution or product.
- *Encouraging collaboration.* Engaging learners in opportunities to work effectively with others is a 21st-century skill. Collaborative activities allow learners to provide peer support when necessary and benefit from the knowledge and skills of other group members.
- *Providing experiential, hands-on tasks.* Experiential activities like simulations, demonstrations, and role-plays serve as contexts for actively using the target language. Interest and engagement increase when more senses are used to complete the activity.
- *Incorporating higher-order thinking.* Incorporating higher-order thinking into tasks in the language classroom encourages learners to analyze, evaluate, and create using the target language. Learners' thinking is extended beyond the comprehension level by requiring them to elaborate with additional details, justify their responses, give examples, and make judgments.

It is helpful for instructors to track how often they use various types of instructional strategies during a week. Table 23 is an observation checklist of the categories of learner engagement. Consider how these strategies are reflected in your lessons over the course of one week. At the end of the week, look at the strategies you used, and rate their effectiveness with a + , √ , -, based on how well the learners responded to the strategy.

IDEA-SHARING
Refer to the observation checklist and share examples from your own classroom instruction repertoire for each one of the strategies.

Using Learner Feedback to Evaluate Instructional Strategies

Learners can provide important feedback on the strategies and activities used in class and how effective they are in helping them meet their learning goals. Asking learners to rate strategy effectiveness empowers them in feeling they can contribute input to the instructional decision-making process and heightens their awareness of their own learning strengths. Table 24 is an example of an instrument that can be used to collect learner feedback on instructional strategies.

Table 23. Observation checklist

Strategy	Mon	Tues	Wed	Thurs	Fri	What you did	+ √ -
Making purpose and instructions clear							
Making real-life connections							
Giving learners choice and control							
Providing challenging but achievable tasks							
Collaborating with others							
Incorporating games and hands-on activities							
Incorporating higher-order thinking							

Table 24. Learner feedback on instructional strategies

Please rate how effective each activity type is in your language learning:				
Pair work	(low) 1	2	3	4 (high)
Choice activities	(low) 1	2	3	4 (high)
Games	(low) 1	2	3	4 (high)
Small group work	(low) 1	2	3	4 (high)
Working independently	(low) 1	2	3	4 (high)
Other suggestions for activities that help you learn?				

The effectiveness of instructional strategies needs to be assessed by both instructor and learners. Instructors tend to use strategies that were successful for them when they were learners and avoid using strategies that did not work for them. Instructors must check in periodically with learners to see what is working for them. Learners often have suggestions about what is helpful for their learning that an instructor may not have considered.

Summary: Successful instructors deliberately reflect on the strategies they have used and how they contribute to learner success in understanding and using the target language. They use a variety of strategies to meet the needs of all learners and to keep the lessons interesting. While there is value in routines, there is also value in innovation. Careful selection of instructional strategies in thoughtfully planned lessons followed by ongoing evaluation of the efficacy of the lessons are requirements for effective classroom instruction.

Reflect on the essential question: How do I evaluate the effectiveness of the strategies I use?

Analyze an example of learner feedback.

Learners in your class completed a feedback form for class and rated the effectiveness of small group work as "low." You know that small group work is important to the development of collaboration skills and for encouraging interactions in the target language.

How would you engage the learners in a discussion about how to improve the effectiveness of small group work?

Apply ideas to your practice using the knowledge gained from the chapter.

It is helpful to have colleagues observe each other's classes. What are some benefits of peer observations? How could you implement peer observations in your school? If you are the only language instructor in your building, consider how you might use videoconferencing software to connect to a partner in another location.

Extend your learning by completing these activities.

1. Think about a lesson you recently taught. Use Pappas' Taxonomy of Reflection chart to respond to the questions about the lesson.

Level of the Taxonomy	Question	Reflection
Remembering	What did I do?	
Understanding	What was important about it? What was the purpose?	
Applying	Where could I use this again? How might I change it?	
Analyzing	Do I see any patterns in what I did?	
Evaluating	How well did I do? What was successful?	
Creating	What should I do next?	

2. Read "What Research Says About Collaborative Inquiry" by Jane David (2008). In the article she describes collaborative inquiry as instructors working together to identify common challenges, analyze relevant data, and test out instructional approaches. Reflect on the potential for collaborative inquiry in your role as an educator.

Deepen your knowledge by exploring additional resources.

Darling-Hammond, L. (2013). *Getting teacher evaluation right: What really matters for effectiveness and improvement.* New York, NY: Teachers College Press.

Little, D. (2005). The Common European Framework and the European Language Portfolio: Involving learners and their judgements in the assessment process. *Language testing, 22*(3), 321-336.

Final Thoughts

The skills of problem-solving, collaboration, creativity, and building relationships are reflected in the concept of Deep Learning, first introduced in 2010 by the William and Flora Hewlett Foundation as a term for the skills and knowledge learners need to succeed in today's world. The American Institutes for Research (AIR, 2015) conducted a study among high schools that were using deep learning strategies and found that learners in these schools had higher scores on standardized tests in mathematics and English, and a higher graduation rate overall.

Michael Fullan & Maria Langworthy, in *A Rich Seam: How New Pedagogies Find Deep Learning* (2014) state:

> Deep learning develops the learning, creating, and doing dispositions that young people need to thrive now and in their futures. Deep learning connects with our core motivations: to directly and deeply engage in learning; and to do things that truly make a difference to our lives and to the world.
>
> The goals of deep learning are that students will gain the competencies and dispositions that will prepare them to be creative, connected, and collaborative life-long problem solvers and to be healthy, holistic human beings who not only contribute to but also create the common good in today's knowledge-based, creative, interdependent world.

The discipline of world languages is the perfect venue for learners to develop these competencies and dispositions as they continue to build their proficiency in communicating with respect and understanding with people from around the world.

Appendix A | World-Readiness Standards

<table>
<tr><th>GOAL AREAS</th><th colspan="3">STANDARDS</th></tr>
<tr><td>COMMUNICATION
Communicate effectively in more than one language in order to function in a variety of situations and for multiple purposes</td><td>Interpersonal Communication:
Learners interact and negotiate meaning in spoken, signed, or written conversations to share information, reactions, feelings, and opinions.</td><td>Interpretive Communication:
Learners understand, interpret, and analyze what is heard, read, or viewed on a variety of topics.</td><td>Presentational Communication:
Learners present information, concepts, and ideas to inform, explain, persuade, and narrate on a variety of topics using appropriate media and adapting to various audiences of listeners, readers, or viewers.</td></tr>
<tr><td>CULTURES
Interact with cultural competence and understanding</td><td>Relating Cultural Practices to Perspectives:
Learners use the language to investigate, explain, and reflect on the relationship between the practices and perspectives of the cultures studied.</td><td colspan="2">Relating Cultural Products to Perspectives:
Learners use the language to investigate, explain, and reflect on the relationship between the products and perspectives of the cultures studied.</td></tr>
<tr><td>CONNECTIONS
Connect with other disciplines and acquire information and diverse perspectives in order to use the language to function in academic and career-related situations</td><td>Making Connections:
Learners build, reinforce, and expand their knowledge of other disciplines while using the language to develop critical thinking and to solve problems creatively.</td><td colspan="2">Acquiring Information and Diverse Perspectives:
Learners access and evaluate information and diverse perspectives that are available through the language and its cultures.</td></tr>
<tr><td>COMPARISONS
Develop insight into the nature of language and culture in order to interact with cultural competence</td><td>Language Comparisons:
Learners use the language to investigate, explain, and reflect on the nature of language through comparisons of the language studied and their own.</td><td colspan="2">Cultural Comparisons:
Learners use the language to investigate, explain, and reflect on the concept of culture through comparisons of the cultures studied and their own.</td></tr>
<tr><td>COMMUNITIES
Communicate and interact with cultural competence in order to participate in multilingual communities at home and around the world</td><td>School and Global Communities:
Learners use the language both within and beyond the classroom to interact and collaborate in their community and the globalized world.</td><td colspan="2">Lifelong Learning:
Learners set goals and reflect on their progress in using languages for enjoyment, enrichment, and advancement.</td></tr>
</table>

Appendix B | NCSSFL/ACTFL Can-Do Proficiency Benchmarks

COMMUNICATION	NOVICE PROFICIENCY BENCHMARK	INTERMEDIATE PROFICIENCY BENCHMARK	ADVANCED PROFICIENCY BENCHMARK
INTERPRETIVE	I can identify the general topic and some basic information in both very familiar and everyday contexts by recognizing practiced or memorized words, phrases, and simple sentences in texts that are spoken, written, or signed.	I can understand the main idea and some pieces of information on familiar topics from sentences and series of connected sentences within texts that are spoken, written, or signed.	I can understand the main message and supporting details on a wide variety of familiar and general interest topics across various time frames from complex, organized texts that are spoken, written, or signed.
INTERPERSONAL	I can communicate in spontaneous spoken, written, or signed conversations on both very familiar and everyday topics, using a variety of practiced or memorized words, phrases, simple sentences, and questions.	I can participate in spontaneous spoken, written, or signed conversations on familiar topics, creating sentences and series of sentences to ask and answer a variety of questions.	I can maintain spontaneous spoken, written, or signed conversations and discussions across various time frames on familiar, as well as unfamiliar, concrete topics, using series of connected sentences and probing questions.
PRESENTATIONAL	***I can*** present information on both very familiar and everyday topics using a variety of practiced or memorized words, phrases, and simple sentences through spoken, written, or signed language.	***I can*** communicate information, make presentations, and express my thoughts about familiar topics, using sentences and series of connected sentences through spoken, written, or signed language.	I can maintain spontaneous spoken, written, or signed conversations and discussions across various time frames on familiar, as well as unfamiliar, concrete topics, using series of connected sentences and probing questions.

Find the complete NCSSFL-ACTFL Can-Do Statements at *actfl.org/global_statements*.

Appendix C | Getting Acquainted Activities

Group Juggle: Learners stand in a circle. Begin by tossing a globe ball to someone in the circle. Tell the learners that they must remember who is receiving the ball they throw, because they will throw the ball to the same person in subsequent rounds. As you throw the ball, greet the person (example: Ciao, Anna). Anna greets the person who threw the ball. Anna then tosses the ball to someone else and greets that person. That person greets the person who threw the ball. The game continues until everyone has had a turn. Now tell the learners you are going to pick up the pace and throw the ball faster. Continue until everyone has had a turn. Tell the learners that they have to complete the game at an even faster pace. You start the game, always throwing to the same person. After three people have thrown the ball, you start a second ball, tossing to the same person. After the new ball has reached three or four people, start a third ball going around the circle. Successful completion is a successful group juggle.

Quick Line-Up: Learners line up alphabetically by first name. Once the line is formed, quickly go down the line with each person saying "My name is (X)." Now tell the learners to line up by birthday (month and day). Next, have the learners line up by how many years they have lived in the city where they are living now. Continue with two or three more line-ups as a way for the learners to get to know each other. Line-ups might include number of years they have played piano, the furthest they have traveled from home in miles, or the number of movies they saw last summer.

Human Bingo: Using a blank bingo sheet, fill in each block with a description of a person. For example, "has 2 brothers" or "has a dog" or "plays guitar" or "loves chocolate" or "likes to play video games," etc. The learners receive the bingo sheets and move around the room asking others, "Do you have 2 brothers?" or "Do you love chocolate?" etc. If the person responds affirmatively, he writes his name in the box on the bingo sheet of the person who asked the question. When someone has signatures in five boxes in a row, it is a "Bingo." Note: Learners can ask only 2 questions of a person. This ensures that the learners move around and talk to a variety of people.

Snowball: Learners write down three facts about themselves on a piece of paper. Next, they stand up with their paper, form a circle, and crumple up the paper. Now it's time for a snowball fight, where learners throw their crumpled paper at each other for 30 seconds. At the end of the snowball fight, each learner grabs a snowball close by, returns to his/her seat, uncrumples the snowball, and reads the description written on it. Learners can read the description aloud and, a. the class can guess who is described; or b. whoever is described can say it is their description.

Lunch Bag: Give each learner a brown lunch bag and tell that person to go home, place three items in the bag that represent him or her and bring it back to school the next day. In class the next day, learners work in groups of four, sharing what is in the bags they brought. A variation is to have the learners guess what each item represents for the learner who is showing the items in his or her bag. Afterward, learners can write a short explanation of the items they brought and what they represent.

Appendix D | Interpersonal Activities

Building Capacity for Interpersonal Speaking

Provide visual support

Images, drawings, and photos, give learners ideas about what to say. Have the learners brainstorm vocabulary and phrases they need in order to carry on a conversation about the image.

Ask either/or questions

Either/or questions provide beginning learners with a choice, making it easier to respond to the question. For example, ask learners if they like winter or summer. Note that, by teaching beginners the word for "because," their short response can extend to short answers: Do you like winter or summer? I like winter because I like to ski.

Have learners sketch some things they can talk about in preparation for a conversation

This technique allows learners time to think about what to say during a conversation.

Interpersonal Speaking

Give me a hint

Tape the name of a different famous person on the back of each learner in the class. Give learners five to ten minutes to ask each other questions to guess their identity. At the end of that time, have learners discuss in their teams who they think they are and why. Have the teams confirm their answers and share successes with the class.

Charade scenes

A learner acts out a sentence pulled from a jar. For example: "I was walking to school when I tripped, fell, and broke my leg." Note that the sentences have to reflect some aspect of the unit theme. After the scene is viewed two times, the other learners work in pairs to recount what they saw. Scenes can be played out with multiple actors to increase the difficulty level.

Three-step interviews

Learners interact in pairs, interviewing each other about a topic. Then, learners take turns sharing what they have learned from their partners with the rest of their cooperative learning group. The group members ask follow-up or clarification questions. The three-step interview helps learners develop listening and language skills while promoting individual accountability (http://www.learnnc.org/lp/pages/4773)

Surveys

Surveys are good ways for learners to move around the room and to engage in conversations in order to find out information that can later be reported to the class.

Speed-dating conversations

Seat learners in two parallel rows with learners facing each other. Learners ask and respond to questions to find common interests or shared opinions. On cue, the learners on one side shift down one desk. Learners continue changing speaking partners as many times as desired. Learners have a limited time to ask someone their questions.

Debates

Learners work in groups to plan a defense of a position on a topic currently in the news (examples: immigration, global warming, college costs, minimum wage, etc.). Two groups come together to defend opposing views. Each group must react spontaneously to what the other says. This is often used to practice Advanced-Level language.

Set up job fair mock interviews

Ahead of time, learners choose a focus career area for which they will interview their classmates. One half of the class act as interviewers and the other half act as interviewees. Halfway through the class, learners switch roles. After the job fair, learners provide feedback to each other about their interviews.

Label the four corners of the room

The corners of the room are labeled with categories or prompts. Learners move to the corner that best represents their preference or opinion. While in their corner groups, learners support their preferences or opinions, and compare and contrast their group's responses with those of the other corner groups. The four corners activity could be used during a unit on seasons and weather. The corners of the room are labeled with the names of the four seasons. Learners move to the corner of the room labeled with their favorite season. In their corner groups, learners pair off and complete an interpersonal task with a partner about why they selected the season and what their activity preferences are during that season.

Interpersonal Writing

Write journal entries for a classmate to read

Asking learners to write in a journal for a classmate, in response to a prompt the teacher gives about the current unit, is a non-threatening way to improve their writing.

Email another learner or keypal

This authentic activity allows learners to engage in real-life interpersonal writing.

Create and maintain a blog

Blogs are a more challenging form of writing, and provide writing practice on a topic of interest to the individual learner. There is space for other learners to comment on the topic in the blog.

Online messaging

There are multiple resources online for creating interactions among language learners. For example, you can send and receive instant messages with anyone using Google Chat or Google Hangouts.

Appendix E Interpretive Activities

Interpretive Listening

Listen for the main idea

Encourage learners to listen ONLY for what they believe is the main point of the passage, by giving them a list of four possibilities in the target language or in English.

Listen for specific details

Ask learners to identify specific vocabulary or tense indicators. Intensive listening is a skill they will often need and use as their language develops.

Podcasts/Audiobooks

These resources are especially helpful for advanced language learners who do not require visual support to support understanding. Several resources are available by Googling Podcasts in (language) or Audiobooks in (language).

Radio

Radio broadcasts of daily news, weather and/or human interest stories are another way to build listening skills. Several resources are available online, such as http://www.live-radio.net/worldwide.shtml

Listen to native speakers

The University of Texas offers listening resources in Spanish, French, Arabic, German, Portuguese, and Hindi. Visit their website at https://www.coerll.utexas.edu/coerll/materials/language-learning-materials

Interpretive Reading/Viewing

Create a QR code gallery walk

The classroom is set up with QR (Quick Response) codes around the room. Each QR code is connected to a website in the target language. Learners gather information from each site in order to create an argument for or against a topic.

Comic Books/Graphic Novels

Comic books and graphic novels combine reading and viewing to facilitate comprehension. Use the images to introduce the story to the learners. Create collages of the images that highlight various aspects of the main characters' personality.

Instructions to assemble/make something

Follow written instructions to make something or assemble something.

Appendix F Presentational Activities

Presentational Speaking

Use the features that accompany PowerPoint

Most learners are comfortable creating presentations using PowerPoint. The Speakers feature may be less familiar. It allows learners to create notes to support an oral presentation they can reference as they give their presentations.

Memorize a dialogue with high-frequency phrases

Unlike spontaneous dialogues that may contain errors, a memorized or prepared dialogue can be error-free with feedback and editing. It gives learners a bank of high-frequency phrases that can be useful when learners move to the Interpersonal Mode where they must speak spontaneously.

Make a presentation grab bag

Fill a bag with objects or topics on strips of paper that relate to the theme of the instructional unit. Learners pull out an item and speak for a minute about it to build their "on-demand" speaking skills.

Present a puppet show

Some learners perform better when they take on a puppet character's role and are not visible to the audience. *Puppet Pals* and *Sock Puppets* are tablet-based apps that create puppet shows.

Demonstrate how to do something

This activity helps learners develop the ability to sequence items. There are many videos available as models to show how to make a dessert, create a scrapbook, pack a suitcase, etc., for learners to watch. These models help them create their own demonstrations.

Create a movie or TV promo

Promos often make use of imperative forms of verbs or superlative forms of adjectives. Many L2 examples are available as models on the Internet.

Presentational Writing

Create a multimedia presentation from a prepared script

Learners use technology to build a presentation and then write, edit, and publish a written script to accompany the presentation.

Write new endings to stories

Learners can use the original ending to a story as a model for creating a new ending.

Write captions under images

This activity is especially good for beginning learners as they use single words, phrases, and short sentences to describe, explain or comment on an image.

Write a fable/story

The fable is a way for learners to explore a cultural product or practice and then create a story to explain the product or practice. Divide the class into small groups. Have learners pass a sheet of paper that contains a simple drawing around the group. Each member adds a feature to a picture. As learners draw on the picture, they describe what they drew in a complete sentence in the target language. Eventually, small groups create stories based on the visual and the explanatory descriptions.

Bibliography and Resources

Ackersold, J. A., & Field, M. L. (1997). *From reader to reading teacher: Issues and strategies for second language classrooms.* New York: Cambridge University Press.

American Council on the Teaching of Foreign Languages (ACTFL). (2011). 21st century skills map. Retrieved from https://www.actfl.org/sites/default/files/pdfs/21stCenturySkillsMap/p21_worldlanguagesmap.pdf

American Council on the Teaching of Foreign Languages (ACTFL). (2015). *ACTFL Performance descriptors for language learners.* Alexandria, VA: ACTFL. Retrieved from http://www.actfl.org/publications/guidelines-and-manuals/actfl-performance- descriptors-language-learners.

American Council on the Teaching of Foreign Languages (ACTFL). (2014). Global competence position statement. Alexandria, VA: ACTFL. Retrieved from https://www.actfl.org/news/position-statements/global-competence-position-statement

American Council on the Teaching of Foreign Languages (ACTFL). (2013). Language as a core component of education for all students. Alexandria, VA: ACTFL. Retrieved from https://www.actfl.org/news/position-statements/languages-core-component-education-all-students

American Council on the Teaching of Foreign Languages (ACTFL). (2010). Language learning for heritage and native speakers. Alexandria, VA: ACTFL. Retrieved from https://www.actfl.org/news/position-statements/language-learning-heritage-and-native-speakers

American Council on the Teaching of Foreign Languages (ACTFL). (2017). NCSSFL-ACTFL Can-Do Statements. Retrieved from https://www.actfl.org/sites/default/files/pdfs/TLE_pdf/OralProficiencyWorkplacePoster.pdf

American Council on the Teaching of Foreign Languages (ACTFL). (n.d.). Oral proficiency levels in the workplace. Retrieved from https://www.actfl.org/sites/default/files/pdfs/TLE_pdf/OralProficiencyWorkplacePoster.pdf

American Council on the Teaching of Foreign Languages (ACTFL). (2017). Role of technology in language learning. Position statement. ACTFL. Retrieved from https://www.actfl.org/news/position-statements/statement-the-role-technology-language-learning

American Council on the Teaching of Foreign Languages (ACTFL). (2010). Use of the target language in the classroom. Alexandria, VA: ACTFL. Retrieved from https://www.actfl.org/news/position-statements/use-the-target-language-the-classroom

Alber, R. (2012, updated 2017). Deeper learning: A collaborative classroom is key [Web log comment]. *George Lucas Educational Foundation: Edutopia.* Retrieved from https://www.edutopia.org/blog/deeper-learning-collaboration-key-rebecca-alber

Anderson, N. (1999). *Exploring second language reading: Issues and strategies.* Boston, MA: Heinle & Heinle.

Augustine, A. (2016). Strategies for better collaboration. *Lifewire.* Retrieved from http://collaboration.about.com/od/basics/a/Strategies-For-Better-Collaboration.htm

Bandura, A. (1986). *Social foundations of thought and action: A social cognitive theory.* Upper Saddle River, NJ: Prentice-Hall, Inc.

Barber, M. (2014). Foreword. In *A Rich Seam: How New Pedagogies Find Deep Learning.* London, UK: Pearson.

Barnford, J., & Day, R. (1998). Extensive reading in the second language classroom. RELC Journal, December 1988, 187-191. doi: 10.1177/003368829802900211

Berne, J. E. (2004) Listening comprehension strategies: A review of the literature. *Foreign Language Annals, 37*, 521-533.

Bernhardt, E. (1991). *Reading development in a second language.* Norwood, NJ: Ablex.

Block, J. (2014). Nurturing collaboration: 5 strategies [Web log comment]. *George Lucas Educational Foundation: Edutopia.* Retrieved from http://www.edutopia.org/blog/nurturing-collaboration-5-strategies-joshua-block

Blythe, T., & Allen, D. (1999). *Looking together at student work: a companion guide to assessing student learning.* New York, NY: Teachers College Press.

Boundless. (2015). Effective Teaching Strategies. Retrieved from https://www.boundless.com/education/textbooks/boundless-education-textbook/working-with-students-4/teaching-strategies-21/effective-teaching-strategies-64-12994/

Bristor, V. J., & Drake, S. V. (1994). Linking the language arts and content areas through visual technology. *THE Journal (Technological Horizons In Education), 22*(2), 74.

Brookfield, S. (1995). *Becoming a critically reflective teacher.* San Francisco, CA: Jossey-Bass.

Brubacher, J. W., & Case, C. W. (1994). *Becoming a reflective educator: How to build a culture of inquiry in the schools.* Thousand Oaks, CA: Corwin Press.

Bruen, J. (2001) Strategies for success: Profiling the effective learner. *Foreign Language Annals, 34*(3), 216-225.

Bruner, J. (1956). *A study of thinking.* New York: Wiley.

Byrnes, H. (1984). The role of listening comprehension: A theoretical base. *Foreign Language Annals, 17,* 317-329.

Carrick, L. U. (2006). Readers Theatre across the curriculum. In T. Rasinski, C. Blachowicz, & K. Lems (Eds.), *Fluency instruction: Research-based best practices* (pp. 209-230). New York, NY: Guilford Press.

Chamot, A. U. (1993). Student responses to learning strategy instruction in the foreign language classroom. *Foreign Language Annals, 26*(3), 308-321.

Chamot, A. U., Barnhardt, S., El-Dinary, P., & Robbins, J. (1999). *The learning strategies handbook.* White Plains, NY: Addison-Wesley Longman.

Chamot, A. U., Barnhardt, S., El-Dinary, P. B., & Robbins, J. (1996). Methods for teaching learning strategies in the foreign language classroom. In R. L. Oxford (Ed.), *Language learning strategies around the world: Cross-cultural perspectives* (pp. 175-187). Honolulu, HI: University of Hawaii Press.

Chamot, A. U., & Kupper, L. (1989). Learning strategies in foreign language instruction. *Foreign Language Annals, 22*(1), 13-24.

Clementi, D., & Sandrock, P. (2011). Conference session: Connecting language with cross-cultural skills for successful collaboration. ACTFL Conference, November 19, 2011.

Clementi, D., & Terrill, L. (2013). *The keys to planning for learning: Effective curriculum, unit, and lesson design.* Alexandria, VA: ACTFL.

Clifford, M. (2011). 20 collaborative learning tips and strategies for teachers. *TeachThought: We grow teachers.* Retrieved from http://www.teachthought.com/pedagogy/20-collaborative-learning-tips-and-strategies/

Cohen, A. D. (1998). *Strategies in learning and using a second language.* London, UK: Longman.

Connell, G. (2014, January 15). Twelve steps to creating a language-rich environment [Web log comment]. *Scholastic.* Retrieved from https://www.scholastic.com/teachers/blog-posts/genia-connell/12-steps-creating-language-rich-environment/

Curtain, H., & Dahlberg, C. (2015). *Languages and learners: Making the match: World language instruction in k-8 classrooms and beyond* (5th ed.). Boston, MA: Pearson.

Dam, L., Legenhausen, L., & Wolff, D. (1990). Text production in the foreign language classroom and the word processor. *System, 18*(3), 325-333.

Danielson, C. (2013). *The framework for teaching: Evaluation instrument* (2013 ed.). Princeton, NJ: Danielson Group.

David, J. L. (2008, December). What research says about collaborative inquiry. *Educational Leadership, 66,* 87-88.

Day, R. R., & Bamford, J. (1998). *Extensive reading in the second language classroom.* New York, NY: Cambridge University Press.

Deming, W. E. (1993). *The new economics for industry, government, education.* Cambridge, MA: Massachusetts Institute of Technology, Center for Advanced Engineering Study.

Denton, P. (2005). *Learning through academic choice.* Turners Falls, MA: Northeast Foundation for Children.

Devine, J. (1993). The role of metacognition in second language reading and writing. In J. G. Carson & I. Leki (Eds.), *Reading in the composition classroom (pp. 105-127).* Boston, MA: Heinle & Heinle.

Dhonau, S. (2014). Personal communication.

Fisher, C. (2011). Using Web 2.0 tools in the language classroom. Calico Spanish. Retrieved from https://calicospanish.com/using-web-2-0-tools-in-the-language-classroom/

Fredricks, J. A., Blumenfeld, P. C., & Paris, A. H. (2004) School engagement: Potential of the concept, state of the evidence. *Review of Educational Research. 74*(1), 59-109.

Freiberg, K., & Freiberg, J. (2016). 17 strategies for improving collaboration. *Resources: Ideas to read and pass along.* Retrieved from http://www.freibergs.com/resources/articles/accountability/17-strategies-for- improving-collaboration/.

Fullan, M., Langworthy, M., & Barber, M. (2014). *A rich seam: How new pedagogies find deep learning.* Boston, MA: Pearson.

Galloway, V. (1992). Toward a cultural reading of authentic texts. In H. Byrnes (Ed.), *Languages for a multicultural world in transition* (pp. 87-121). Lincolnwood, IL: National Textbook Co.

Glazer, S. M. (1992). *Reading comprehension: Self-monitoring strategies to develop independent readers.* New York, NY: Scholastic Professional Books.

Glazer, S. M., & Brown, C. S. (1993). *Portfolios and beyond: Collaborative assessment in reading and writing.* Norwood, MA: Christopher-Gordon Publishers.

Great Schools Partnership. (2016). Glossary of education reform. *Great Schools Partnership.* Retrieved from http://www.greatschoolspartnership.org/resources/glossary-of-education-reform/

Green, J. M., & Oxford, R. (1995). A closer look at learning strategies, L2 proficiency, and gender. *TESOL Quarterly*, *29*, 261-297.

Gregory, G., & Kuzmich, L. (2004). *Data driven differentiation in the standards-based classroom.* Thousand Oaks, CA: Corwin Press.

Griffith, L. W., & Rasinski, T. (2004). A focus on fluency: How one teacher incorporated fluency with her reading curriculum. *The Reading Teacher*, *58*(2), 126-133.

Halverson, E. R., & Sheridan, K. M. (2014). The maker movement in education: Designing, creating, and learning across contexts. *Harvard Educational Review, Winter 2014.* Retrieved from http://hepg.org/her-home/issues/harvard-educational-review-volume-84-number-4/herarticle/symposium

Harris, K. (2010). *World languages standards* (2nd ed.). Arlington, VA: National Board for Professional Teaching Standards.

Hauck, B., & Glisan, E. (2013). *Implementing integrated performance assessment.* Alexandria, VA: American Council on the Teaching of Foreign Languages.

Holec, H. A. (1981). *Autonomy and foreign language learning.* Oxford, UK: Pergamon.

Hunter, M. (1982). *Mastery teaching.* El Segundo, CA: TIP Publications.

Jackson, R., & Zmuda, A. (2014). Four (Secret) Keys to Student Engagement. *Educational Leadership*, *72*(1), 18-24.

Jensen, E. (2005). *Teaching with the brain in mind* (2nd ed.). Alexandria, VA. ASCD.

Kaemena360. (n.d.). Retrieved from http://www.kaemena360.com/

Kagan, S., & Kagan, M. (2009). *Kagan cooperative learning.* Moorabbin, Vic.: Hawker Brownlow Education.

Kim, L. S. (1995). Creative games for the language class. *FORUM Online,* 33(1), 35. Retrieved from http://dosfan.lib.uic.edu/usia/E-USIA/forum/vols/vol33/no1/P35.htm

King, A. (1993). From sage on the stage to guide on the side. *College Teaching*, *41*(1), 30-35.

Koning, P. (2011). Language can be music to students' ears. *The Language Educator*, *February 2011,* 32-36. Retrieved from https://www.actfl.org/sites/default/files/pdfs/TLEsamples/TLE_Feb11_Article.pdf

Krashen, S. D. (1982). *Principles and practice in second language acquisition*. Oxford, UK: Pergamon Press.

Krashen, S. D. (1981). *Second language acquisition and second language learning.* Oxford, UK: Pergamon Press.

Krashen, S. D. (1988). *Second language acquisition and second language learning* (2nd ed.). Upper Saddle River, NJ: Prentice-Hall.

#LangChat. (2012). Strategies for staying in the target language with beginners. *Calico Spanish.* Retrieved from http://blog.calicospanish.com/2012/10/19/strategies-for- staying-in-the-target-language-with-beginners.html#sthash.EfzQdwyE.dpuf

Larmer, J., & Mergendoller, J. R. (2010). Seven essentials for project-based learning. *Educational Leadership*, *68*(1), 34-37. Retrieved from http://www.ascd.org/publications/educational_leadership/sept10/vol68/num01/Seven_Essentials_for_Project-Based_Learning.aspx

LeLoup, J. W., & Ponterio, R. (2000). Creating standards-based activities integrating authentic materials from the WWW. In W. Heller (Ed.), *ABC to PhD: Foreign Language Proficiency for ALL*, Annual Meeting Series No. 17 (pp. 13-20). Schenectady, NY: New York State Association of Foreign Language Teachers.

Lesson Study Research Group. (n.d.). What is lesson study? Teachers College, Columbia University. New York, NY. Retrieved from http://www.tc.columbia.edu/lessonstudy/lessonstudy.html.

Lightbown, P. (2016). All in good time: making classroom minutes count. *Sixth Annual Conference on Immersion and Dual Language Education, October 20, 2016.* Minneapolis, MN: Center for Advanced Research on Language Acquisition.

Lightbown, P., & Spada, N. M. (2006). *How languages are learned.* Oxford University Press, USA.

Little, D. (2009). Language learner autonomy and the European language portfolio: Two L2 English examples. *Language Teaching, 42*(02), 222-233.

Little, D. (2003). Learner autonomy and second/foreign language learning. In CIEL Language Support Network (Eds.), *The guide to good practice for learning and teaching in languages, linguistics and area studies* [electronic]. Retrieved from https://www.researchgate.net/publication/259874624_Learner_autonomy_and_secondforeign_language_learning

Locke, E. A., & Latham, G. P. (1990). *A theory of goal setting & task performance.* Upper Saddle River, NJ: Prentice-Hall, Inc.

Lund, R. J. (1990). A taxonomy for teaching second language listening. *Foreign Language Annals, 23*, 105-115.

Lynch, T. (1998). Theoretical perspectives on listening. *Annual Review of Applied Linguistics, 18,* 3-19.

Lyster, R., & Ballinger, S. (2011). Content-based language teaching: Convergent concerns across divergent contexts. *Language Teaching Research, 15*(3), 279-288.

MacIntyre, P. D. (2007). Willingness to communicate in the second language: Understanding the decision to speak as a volitional process. *The Modern Language Journal, 91*, 564-576.

Maryland State Department of Education. (2016). Introduction to the Classroom-Focused Improvement Process (CFIP). *School Improvement in Maryland.* Retrieved from http://mdk12.org/process/cfip/index.html.

Marzano, R. J. (2013). Art and science of teaching / Ask yourself: Are students engaged? *Educational Leadership: Technology-Rich Learning, 70*(6), 81-82. Retrieved from http://www.ascd.org/publications/educational-leadership/mar13/vol70/num06/Ask-Yourself@-Are-Students-Engaged%C2%A2.aspx

Marzano, R. J. (2017). Dr. Robert Marzano's suite. Retrieved from http://www.iobservation.com/Marzano-Suite/

Marzano. R. J. (2010). Using games to enhance student achievement. *Education Leadership, 67*(5), 71-72. Retrieved from http://www.ascd.org/publications/educational_leadership.aspx

Marzano, R. J., Pickering, D. J., & Heflebower, T. (2010) *The highly engaged classroom: The classroom strategies series (Generating high levels of student attention and engagement).* Bloomington, IN: Marzano Research Laboratory.

Marzano, R. J., Pickering, D.J., & Pollock, J. E. (2001). *Classroom instruction that works: Research-based strategies for increasing student achievement* (2nd ed.). Boston, MA: Pearson.

McCarthy, M., & O'Keeffe, A. (2004). Research in the teaching of speaking. *Annual Review of Applied Linguistics, 24*, 26-43.

Mendelsohn, D. J., & Rubin, J. (1995). *A guide for the teaching of second language listening.* San Diego, CA: Dominie Press.

Meyer, B., Haywood, N., Sachdev, D., & Faraday, S. (2008). *What is independent learning, and what are the benefits for students?* London, UK: Department for Children, Schools and Families Research Report 051.

Micken, P. (2013). *Language curriculum design and socialization.* Bristol: Multilingual Matters.

Moeller, A. J. (2005). *Documenting and improving student learning through the LinguaFolio* (Unpublished doctoral dissertation). University of Nebraska-Lincoln, Lincoln, NE.

Moeller, A. J. & Nugent, K. (2014). Building intercultural competence in the language classroom. In S. Dhonau (Ed.), *Unlock the gateway to communication: 2014 report of the Central States Conference on the Teaching of Foreign Languages* (pp. 1-18). Richmond, VA: Robert M. Terry. Retrieved from http://www.csctfl.org/documents/2014Report/CSCTFLReport2014.pdf

Moeller, A. J., Theiler, J. M., & Wu, C. (2012). Goal setting and student achievement: A longitudinal study. *The Modern Language Journal, 96*(2), 153-169.

Moeller, A. J., & Yu, F. (2015). NCSSFL-ACTFL Can-Do statements: An effective tool for improving language learning within and outside the classroom. *Dimension, 50*, 69.

Morain, G. (1986). *The role of culture in foreign language education* (ERIC Document 276298). Washington, DC: ERIC Clearinghouse on Languages and Linguistics. Ret

Morain, G. (1976). Visual literacy: Reading signs and designs in the foreign culture. *Foreign Language Annals, 9*(3), 210-216.

National Council of State Supervisors for Languages (NCSSFL) & American Council on the Teaching of Foreign Languages (ACTFL). (2013). NCSSFL-ACTFL Can-Do statements. Alexandria, VA: ACTFL. Retrieved from https://www.actfl.org/publications/guidelines-and-manuals/ncssfl-actfl-can-do-statements

National School Reform Faculty. (2014). Frequently asked questions: What is a Critical Friends Group® (CFG®) community and how is it different than a PLC? *National School Reform Faculty Harmony Education Center.* Retrieved from https://www.nsrfharmony.org/about-us/faq

National Standards in Foreign Language Education Project (NSFLEP). (2006). *Standards for foreign language learning in the 21st century (SFLL).* Lawrence, KS: Allen Press.

NCTE position statement on literacy (2013, February). NCTE Comprehensive News. Retrieved from http://www.ncte.org/positions/literacy.

Newmann, F. M. & Associates (1996). *Authentic achievement: Restructuring schools for intellectual quality.* San Francisco, CA: Jossey-Bass.

Nunan, D., & Miller, L. (Eds.). (1995). *New ways in teaching listening.* Alexandria, VA: TESOL.

Ogle, D. (1986). K-W-L: A teaching model that develops active reading of expository text. *The Reading Teacher*, *39*, 564-570.

O'Malley, M. J., & Chamot, A. U. (1990). *Learning strategies in second language acquisition.* Cambridge, UK: Cambridge University Press.

Open Educational Resources in World Languages. http://www.recovery.gov/Pages/default.aspx

Oxford, R. L. (2008). Hero with a thousand faces: Learner autonomy, learning strategies and learning tactics in independent language learning. *Language learning strategies in independent settings*, 41-63.

Oxford, R. L. (1990). *Language learning strategies: What every teacher should know.* New York, NY: Newbury House.

Paesani, K., Allen, H. W., & Dupuy, B. A. (2015). *Multiliteracies framework for collegiate foreign language teaching.* Upper Saddle River, NJ: Pearson.

Pappas, P. (2010). The reflective teacher: A taxonomy of reflection, part 3. *Copy/Paste.* Retrieved from http://peterpappas.com/2010/01/reflective-teacher-taxonomy-reflection.html

Partnership for 21st Century Learning. (n.d.). Retrieved from http://www.p21.org/index.php

Performance Assessment & Common Core | Exemplars. http://www.exemplars.com/. Retrieved August 15, 2014.

Perks, K. (2010, March 1). Crafting Effective Choices to Motivate Students. *Adolescent Literacy in Perspective.* Columbus, OH: Ohio Resource Center.

Phillips, J. K., & Abbott, M. (2011). A decade of foreign language standards: Influence, impact, and future directions (2011): Alexandria, VA: ACTFL. Retrieved from https://www.actfl.org/sites/default/files/publications/standards/NationalStandards2011.pdf

Pikulski, J. J., & Chard, D. J. (2005). Fluency: Bridge between decoding and reading comprehension. *The Reading Teacher, 58*(6), 510-519.

Pinterest. (n.d.). Infographics—many languages. *Pinterest.* Retrieved from https://www.pinterest.com/csctfl/infographics-many-languages/.

Popham, W. J. (2011). *Transformative assessment in action: An inside look at applying the process.* Alexandria, VA: ASCD.

Prensky, M. R. (2012). *From digital natives to digital wisdom: Hopeful essays for 21st century learning.* Thousand Oaks, CA: Corwin Press.

Puentedura, R. (2010). *Ruben R. Puentedura's blog: Ongoing thoughts on education and technology.* Retrieved from http://www.hippasus.com/rrpweblog/

Rebora, A. (2008). Making a difference: Carol Ann Tomlinson explains how differentiation works and why we need it now. *Education Week PD Teacher Sourcebook*, *2*(26), 28-31.

Robbins, P. (1991). *How to plan and implement a peer coaching program.* Alexandria, VA: Association for Supervision and Curriculum Development.

Robinson, A., Silver, H., & Strong, R. (September 1995). Strengthening student engagement: What do students want? *Educational Leadership*, *53*, 8-12. Alexandria, VA: Association for Supervision and Curriculum Development.

Rost, M. (2002). Listening tasks and language acquisition. In *Memorias del Congreso JALT (Japan Association of Language Teachers) 2002* (pp. 18-28). Retrieved from http://latcomm.com/2012/11/listening-tasks-and-language-acquisition/

Rubin, J. (1995). The contribution of video to the development of competence in listening. In D. J. Mendelsohn & J. Rubin (Eds.), *A guide for the teaching of second language listening* (pp. 151-165). San Diego, CA: Dominie Press.

Sandrock, P. (2010). *The keys to assessing language performance.* Alexandria, VA. ACTFL.

Santa, C. (1988). *Content reading including study systems.* Dubuque, IA: Kendall/Hunt Publishing.

Schlechty, P. (2002). *Working on the Work.* Indianapolis, IN: Jossey-Bass.

Shrum, J. L., & Glisan, E. W. (2016). *Teacher's handbook, contextualized language instruction.* Boston, MA: Cengage Learning.

Silberstein, S. (1994). *Techniques and resources in teaching reading.* New York, NY: Oxford University Press.

Slavin, R. E. (1987). Cooperative learning and the cooperative school. *Educational Leadership*, *45*(3), 7-13.

Sousa, D. A., & Tomlinson, C. A. (2011). *Differentiation and the brain: How neuroscience supports the learner-friendly classroom.* Bloomington, IN: Solution Tree Press.

Spada, N., & Lightbown, P. M. (2008). Form-focused instruction: Isolated or integrated? *Tesol Quarterly*, 181-207.

Srinivas, H. (n.d.). Four Collaborative Learning Strategies. *The Global Development Research Center.* Retrieved from http://www.gdrc.org/kmgmt/c-learn/strategies.html

Stevick, W. (1976). *Memory, meaning, and method.* Boston, MA: Heinle & Heinle.

Swaffar, J., Arens, K., & Byrnes, H. (1991). *Reading for meaning: An integrated approach to language learning.* Englewood Cliffs, NJ: Prentice-Hall.

Swender, E., Conrad, D. J., & Vicars, R. (2012). *ACTFL proficiency guidelines-speaking, writing, listening and reading.* 3rd ed. Alexandria, VA: American Council on the Teaching of Foreign Languages. Retrieved from https://www.actfl.org/sites/default/files/pdfs/public/ACTFLProficiencyGuidelines2012_FINAL

Tell Project. (n.d.). Teacher effectiveness for language learning framework. *Teacher Effectiveness for Language Learning.* Retrieved from http://www.tellproject.org/framework/

Tewksbury, B.J., & McDonald, R. (2017). Teaching Strategies. Retrieved from https://serc.carleton.edu/NAGTWorkshops/coursedesign/tutorial/strategies.html

Theisen, T., Fulton-Archer, L., Smith, M. J., Sauer, T., Small, H., & Abbott, M. (2011). *21st century skills map.* Washington, DC: American Council for the Teaching of Foreign Languages. Retrieved from http://www.actfl.org/sites/default/files/pdfs/21stCenturySkillsMap/p21_ worldlanguagesmap.pdf

The National Standards Collaborative Board. (2015). *World-Readiness Standards for Learning Languages.* 4th ed. Alexandria, VA: Author.

Tierney, R. J., Carter, M. A., & Desai, L. E. (1991). *Portfolio assessment in the reading-writing classroom.* Norwood, MA: Christopher-Gordon Publishers.

Tomlinson, C. A. (2001). *How to differentiate instruction in mixed-ability classrooms* (2nd ed.). Alexandria, VA: Association for Supervision and Curriculum Development.

Tomlinson, C. A. (2000). Reconcilable differences: Standards-based teaching and differentiation. *Educational Leadership, 58*(1), 6-13. Retrieved from https://eric.ed.gov/?id=EJ614602

Tomlinson, C. A. (1999). *The differentiated classroom responding to the needs of all learners.* Alexandria, VA: Association for Supervision and Curriculum Development.

Tomlinson, C. A., & Allan, S. D. (2000). *Leadership for differentiating schools and classrooms.* Alexandria, VA. ASCD.

Transparent Language. (2013). 7 ways to develop good habits in language learning [Web log comment]. *Transparent Language.* Retrieved from http://blogs.transparent.com/language-news/2013/09/09/7-ways-to-develop-good-habits-in-language-learning/

Tyson, R. E. (1998). 'Serious' fun: Using games, jokes, and stories in the language classroom. Daejin University, Summer Workshop for Elementary School Teachers, August 1998. Retrieved from http://english.daejin.ac.kr/~rtyson/cv/games.html.

Urquhart, A. H., & Weir, C. (1998). *Reading in a second language: Process, product, and practice.* New York, NY: Longman.

Vandergrift, L. (2007). Recent developments in second and foreign language listening comprehension research. *Language Teaching, 40,* 191-210. doi:10.1017/S0261444807004338

Warschauer, M. (2007). The paradoxical future of digital learning. *Learning Inquiry, 1*(1), 41-49.

Wiggins, G. P., & McTighe, J. (1998). *Understanding by design.* Alexandria, VA. ASCD.

Young, C., & Rasinski, T. (2009). Implementing Readers Theatre as an approach to classroom fluency instruction. *The Reading Teacher, 63*(1), 4-13.

Ziegler, N. A., & Moeller, A. J. (2012). Increasing self-regulated learning through the LinguaFolio. *Foreign Language Annals, 45*(3), 330-348.